Inspiration

The title of the book "Stranger In This World" is inspired from the song written by Boy George from the Musical Taboo, I would like to encourage you to look up the lyrics.

This book is dedicated to my mum Ruth Garlington, who is my rock, best friend and Mother. The first person to love me unconditionally in all I turn my hand to, without judgement or limitation. Thank you for being the person you are and guiding me forward and being my constant Star when I have found myself a stranger in this world.

The love between a son and their mother is untouchable, unbreakable, bound together for all eternity with invisible golden threads of light.

Love you always now and forever.

Your Son x

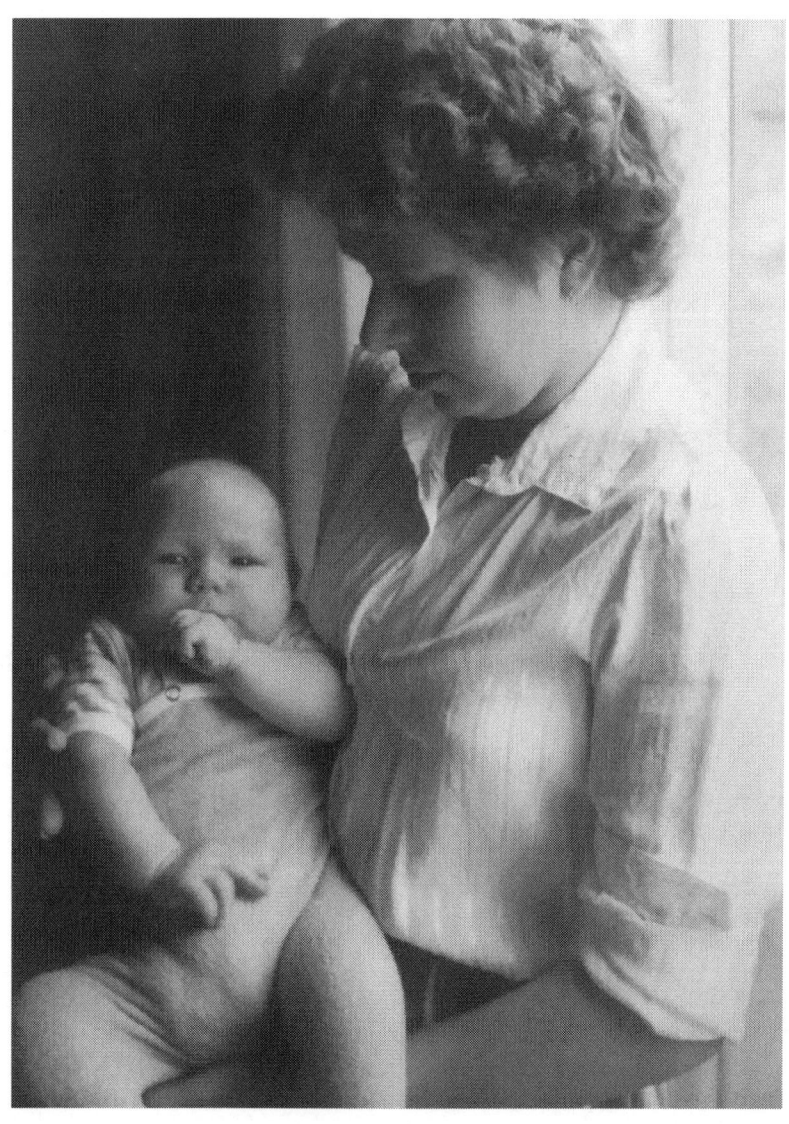

Unconditional Love

Introduction

Michael Garlington, Born in Bath Royal United Hospital at 8.00 pm on Sunday 19th of January 1986. Brought up in the sleepy town of Frome, Somerset, (since revamped and is now one of the most desirable towns to live in). Weighing in at eight pounds. Known to most people as "Mitch".

This is my story of how I came to be the person I am today. Spiritual Medium, Psychic, Tarot Reader, Healer, Male Witch. Hopefully you will see that I am just a regular guy, living an interesting if not slightly alternative way of life.

I have never been one of those people that wanted to 'fit in' or be 'normal'. What's normal?

> Normal is illusion. What is normal to the spider is chaos to the fly. - *Mortica Adams*

Those that know me, know I have an air of Mystic and Magic about me. This has never been put on, it's simply a part of me. I guess that's the Witch in me?

Why write a book? Because friends, family, clients and most importantly the Spirit World have been on at me for some time now! There had to be a starting point ... So, this is it.

I hope I can share with you my experiences both from the spiritual walk of life, but also the everyday physical world in which we have to live in. Things I have learnt along the way, that have shaped and made me the person I am today, on my journey so far.

My aim is that if part of my own adventure or past can reach out and help, encourage, influence or bring fresh hope and a renewed sense of self-worth to one person, this book will have been worth writing.

Affirmation

Life is a never-ending road, full of twists and turns. We laugh and cry, we learn and grow all the time. Enjoy the journey, forget the past it is done. Don't worry about the future it is yet to come. Focus on the now. That feeling of being alive and at one with the world. For life is the greatest gift you will ever receive. - *Mitch Garlington*

Growing Up

I guess we must travel back in time to understand the now... something I have put off doing for a long time. This book is not just about you the reader, it's also about me being able to share good and bad experiences, locking them in the chapters and being able to smile that I have survived and can pass on the tales from previous times in my life.

I am often asked by clients and others, 'When did you first work with spirit?' 'How did you know you had the gift?' and all the other questions that go with it. Well... the truth is I have always been working with spirit, I just didn't realise it back then. Some people need to be 'convinced' or have some big awakening that there is an afterlife. From as far back as I can remember, I always knew in my heart of hearts there were other worlds and realms.

It really was a feeling so deep within me, I took it as matter of fact, second nature - it was just the way it was. Growing up, certain people around me shared more 'black and white' belief systems - when you die that's it you die! I found this to be so cold and unattached from the world and how I saw and knew it. The vessel we travel in does indeed give up and close down. But the spirit, that universal soul or energy which makes me, me, and you, you very much lives on. But we will learn more about that later.

Childhood was an interesting time for me to say the least. I have been blessed with the most AMAZING family, a Mum and Dad that love me unconditionally and have always done their best for me, and a sister who whilst can be a pain is also more of a best friend, a rock and I would be lost without her. Family life has, on the whole always been good and for that reason I feel truly blessed.

I always knew from a very young age I was different ... I didn't know how, what, or why. But I knew I wasn't like the other kids. Most people my age were quite content kicking a ball around a park or field - I never got it, and still don't to this day. It bores the hell out of me, I don't really like or care for the aggression sport in general seems to bring out in some people, and the absurd amount of money sportspeople get paid. For me Doctors and nurses should receive that kind of pay cheque! They save lives daily, that in itself is a miracle ... not a cocky egotistical kid kicking a ball around a field. (But hey, don't get me started)

Whilst other kids were off living it up in the field, I was quite happy hanging out with the girls, playing with their dolls, sharing stories and talking about every subject under the sun. This to me felt normal and comfortable. I could be myself and it didn't matter. I have always felt a lot older than I am, an old soul on young shoulders so I think that's why I gravitated towards the females around me. They tended to be a bit more mature, whereas the guys seemed to be lacking in brain cells, or so I felt.

From the age of about four, I always felt drawn to Witches, Wizards, Unicorns and Dragons and all the magic they bring with them. My favourite books as I grew a little older were the Worst Witch stories by Jill Murphy. I also had the film on VHS Video and this was a favourite to play. So much so, parts of the tape would get stuck in the machine and you had to rewind the tape with your fingers to get it to play.

It sounds a little unusual, but I always felt I was a witch. It was never something I had to question it was simple fact. I would often wave my hands around in mystical gestures in the hope that one day I might become invisible, or fly, or any kind of magical power to happen. Whilst that never did, I did sometimes feel like my incantations had been heard and it made me feel a little better within myself.

Whilst I can't remember this as I was too young, I was also apparently mad about cars when I was starting to talk, and I could name random cars that were shown to me. Not just one or two, ten to twenty different makes and models and I would know them all off by heart. I did have a lot of toy cars when I was young, but quickly lost interest.

As I became a little older these soon changed to 'Monster in Your Pocket' toys, and certain Lego sets. I was mad on Lego, my parents bought me a HUGE Lego castle and for quite some years that had pride and place in my bedroom.

Disney and pantomimes also played a big part of my childhood days. We would often stick a video on, Snow White, Sleeping Beauty, Cinderella - we loved them all. Every time I would be drawn to the villain or evil character - they were the outcast, the freak, the underdog, so naturally it felt right I wanted them to win even if their intention wasn't great. They always had the most glamorous outfits and stage presence - you knew they were in the room. They were larger than life, had magical powers, tended to be Witches or Sorcerers and I wanted to be like them.

Christmas time growing up was great we often went to see the pantomimes in Bath at the Theatre Royal. When I was younger my sister was too scared to go, so she would stay with Dad. It's only when she got older, she felt she wanted to come along. Pantomimes were something me and Mum did with my Nan (Mum's mum). I used to get so excited seeing these shows I would almost make myself ill with excitement beforehand. Imagine someone that's had too many sweets and OD'd on sugar and gone hyper, that was me. As I got older this calmed down a little, but I still get a little more excited than most seeing any kind of show or performance.

One year I think I was six or seven they played Snow White & The Seven Dwarfs and we had to go so Mum and Nan booked tickets. Whilst I had seen pantomimes before I hadn't always remembered them for very long - but this one stood out for all the right reasons. Not only were we off to see a favourite fairy tale, we had posh seats. As a rule, we would buy seats in the upper circle, but not this time, I believe Nan put some money towards the tickets, so we went for dress circle. This meant you could see the actors faces a little more clearly, we had a little more leg room, and the seats had a bit more padding. Mum and Nan had done good.

The Wicked Queen or "Red Queen" as she was cast was played by the late Marti Caine. This was the first time a pantomime villain really caught my attention. Not only did she have a powerhouse voice and dazzling costumes, she really played the character, her acting was outstanding in this production and I still remember it clearly today. I actually felt really scared at the time that she was going to get me and put me in her big cauldron that was smoking with dry ice on the stage.

I believe this was also one of Bath's pantos with a bigger than usual budget - you could see that they had pulled out all the stops. Needless to say, for the next few months I spent time pretending to be the 'Red Queen' at every chance I had. When we had seen the pantomime, we would take my Nan home. It just so happened she had a big Cauldron style dish that she was going to get rid of to a charity shop. This became my witchy cauldron from childhood days and I made lots of spells and potions with it.

School days were an interesting time. My primary and first school I enjoyed - I was known for being the weird kid, but I quite liked that. I had a friend at the time called Kristy and we literally did everything together. There was no funny business or anything of that nature! We were just kids, and really good mates! She was a bit of a tomboy and saw herself as an outsider too, so didn't always fit into the typical group types of people. I was pretty feminine and flamboyant so struggled with the regular boys and the set up worked quite well. Together we enjoyed and survived first school, I think if I hadn't had Kristy around things may have been different - we kept each other safe and grounded.

These memories were happy times, I look back and smile on these days. Life just seemed a simpler time. The world went a little slower and everyone was a bit gentler on each other.

Me and My Sister Hazel Just Witching Around

A Witch is Born

Whilst Kristy and I were different, we also shared a lot in common. We liked similar music, TV programmes and films so it was easy to talk to her. We would come to school on a Monday and often catch up about things we had seen Simon & The Witch, Grotbags, Teabags and all the other witchy kids programmes from that time. Like me, she was also big into Witches and the unknown.

St Johns First School in Frome was a lovely little school - we used to have an assembly session every day. This would be where all classes in our year got together in the hall. We sat on the floor cross-legged for what seemed like an eternity but was probably about half an hour. A few hymns would be sung out of tune from a choice of hymn books. There was a green and blue one, I can't remember which one now but the hymns in one of the books were a lot more interesting and I used to hope it was the catchy ones we would sing.

Where the hall was situated there was a massive window from floor to ceiling. This overlooked St John's Church in Frome. It looked like the roof of the church was right in front of you. At the top stood a golden cockerel weathervane. Whilst assembly was on I very rarely paid attention to what was being said. I wasn't being rude, I didn't really feel I needed to know whatever they were waffling on about. I would often get lost in my own little day dream or conversations in my head.

I kept thinking how shiny this weathervane looked, and would often wonder how it was cleaned? I saw no stairs or anyway of getting to the peak of the church. 'How was it maintained so nice?' I often wondered.

Suddenly my attention was drawn back into the assembly room, World Book Day had been announced. This was where they turned the assembly hall into a pop-up library and bookshop and you got to dress up as your favourite character from your favourite book. This meant a few things for me. Firstly, parents were encouraged to buy their kids a new book. Secondly, with all kids being dressed up chances were no real work happened and it was more a day of having fun which was always a bonus.

We got up from the hard floor with a numb bum and legs that felt like they had become solid, pins and needles stabbing you whilst you walked back to class. Everyone started deciding what character they were going to be - for me there was no question! I loved the Worst Witch and I identify with the character Mildred Hubble on so many levels. People started asking me what I was going to go as, as I started telling them, everyone seemed a bit shocked and surprised, and slightly dismissive! Why couldn't I go as this character? Because it's a female? Isn't that the whole point of fancy dress, you take on the role of a character? I didn't really understand or have patience for peoples' negative mindset on my character idea. 'Why were they so bothered or worried', I thought, 'focus on your own outfit!' I loved back then and still do now the illusion of fancy dress, when it is done correctly.

I went home and told Mum about what we had to do and that we needed a costume for the following week. Mum has always been very supportive of my creative ways and in all that I do. She thought this was a brilliant idea and got to work on making the outfit. The only condition was that we don't involve or tell Dad too much about what we were up to. This suited me fine as although I loved my Dad I felt as though I was having to explain myself a lot as I was getting older. This didn't and still doesn't sit well with me.

Mum made an amazing outfit and we borrowed my sister's grey school dress, as she was in the year below – a little tight but we made it fit. Mum made fake hair out of wool and attached it to a witch's hat. She also made a cape with sequin appliqués on the back. That was it, I was set to go. Broomstick with black cat stuffed toy stitched on and satchel in tow, off I went for World Book Day.

Everyone seemed amazed that I pulled it off. But there was no real negative or nasty feedback, in fact I think people were quite impressed. Even the teachers said to my Mum at the end of the day, your kid has some balls to go around like that.

That was just it, at that time in my life I felt free, so comfortable with myself, I didn't care what others thought! why did I need to? I was not ruled by anyone's limitations. For the most part St Johns School was a happy time for me. Whilst I wasn't the most popular kid, I wasn't bullied and had some friends both male and female. I was able to grow and blossom. For me that was enough, what more did I need?

Early Drag Diva in The Making

Stay Awake

Whilst I know I'm not the cleverest of people, I like to think I'm not stupid! However, this was questioned one day when at St John's. I met my Mum in the school playground at the end of a day which was standard practice. The Mums all stood together for a chinwag waiting for their kids to come out and go home.

I came out of class and I was hobbling a little. "Everything alright?" Mum said. "Yes fine" I explained "apart from for some reason my feet are really hurting". She looked down and unknown to me I had my shoes on the wrong feet, oops! She seemed shocked then floods of laughter then shocked again, that I had walked around all day with my shoes on the wrong feet and had not noticed. She still talks about this story now.

It was becoming apparent that certain school subjects were not really for me. I loved English but really struggled with spelling and grammar. I am dyslexic in both writing and numbers, although it's not common knowledge and I try not to let this hold me back. Maths was the worst subject for me, I just did not get it. I often would go into my own little daydreams with this subject.

I was starting to become increasingly tired after school. I was having day dreams that were becoming more 'full on' and I felt like I was almost leaving my body. What was happening was I was going off astral travelling. This was my earliest memories of connecting with the spirit world.

Although I didn't know they were spirits I just thought they were lovely people coming to take me away from the boredom of the class for a while. I was always sent back before the lesson finished. The teacher had no idea what was going on.

As time went on, a meeting was called, the School were concerned that my attention was lagging too much and suggested I might need to be moved back a year. It was also suggested that maybe I was partially deaf, so a test was carried out, everything came back normal and I basically just had to fight and work through it. Mum was very reluctant to put me back a year, she made sure that I stuck it out for my own good. Eventually as I got into a routine the astral travel stopped for a while, and I wasn't so sleepy. I had survived the boredom and was getting on with it. Numbers were and still are a mystery to me, but I plodded on the best I could.

PE was another subject that I didn't really have much time for. The dreaded sports day reared its ugly head once more as it did every year. Egg and spoon race, sack race and so on. 'When would I need these in the real world?' I thought. The only bonus with this was that they made it an all-day affair. We did it at Victoria Park in Frome which was a little walk away from the School itself. 'Brilliant, waste some time' I thought. We all walked in twos so obviously me and Kristy walked together chatting about things that had nothing to do with the task in hand. Parents were roped in to help and it was frowned upon if they didn't get involved! So, Mum was pottering about in the background with all the other mums that didn't really want to be there and had a million other things they could have been doing.

Once at Victoria Park the register was called to check no kids had gone astray. This was a performance in itself, after the eighth time and all teachers happy that all kids were in fact there we got put into teams. There was a Scottish teacher called Ms Sawyers who had her little cliques of people. She taught English and Maths and didn't have much time for me, the feeling was mutual. I thought she was an evil dragon and didn't like her style of teaching at all. It was more like bullying.

She started putting us into groups and put me with all the deadwood, with the rejects and outsiders from other classes. Me and Kristy got split up straight away, much to Ms Sawyer's delight. Well... I was outraged, it wasn't the best way to motivate someone that already wasn't thrilled to be balancing an egg on a spoon on a Friday afternoon. I was missing art for this rubbish, a subject I really enjoyed and was good at.

Ms Sawyer decided she would encourage and guide the loser team herself, I think she felt she could make, mould and turn us into athletes! We had a team talk, and whilst I was not great at PE, I was one of the fastest in my year at running, I really enjoyed cross country running. Ms Sawyer wanted to use that to her advantage and help to win against the other teams. I like to think karma played a big part here, as whilst I was amazingly fast, not so much with an egg and spoon in my hand.

Off we went, and I struggled to keep the egg where it needed to be, getting through about five or six in total. I decided I had more control if I did a power walk. "Run Michael Run!" where the words foaming from her lips. ('fuck off'... was what I thought to myself). When I came back for the next team player to go, all chances of winning were lost due to me losing so many eggs up and back down the track. She looked at me and I just smiled, she knew I had gone deliberately slow, and she would be out for revenge. I didn't care - it made up for all the times she had talked down to me in maths class.

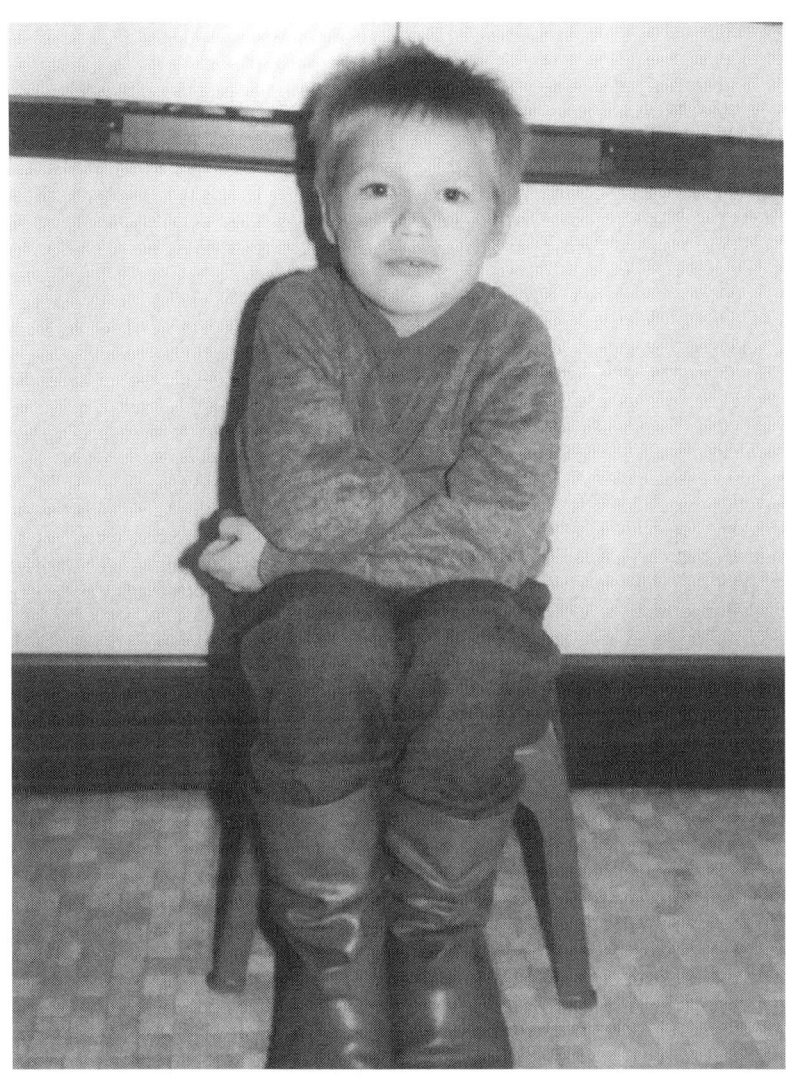

Too Busy Being Fabulous to Worry About the Demands of School

The Music's No Good Without You

Music has always played a massive part of my life, I think it has been the one thing that has often kept me sane in my moments of darkness. Both as a child and through adulthood I have always been interested in many different styles and types of artist. Growing up my main idols were Cher, Donna Summer, Yazz, Shakespeare's Sister – and others came along a little later.

Again, it wasn't just the vocal performance, all these artists put on a show and had stage presence. Cher Live at the Mirage was shown on BBC1 late one evening. Mum recorded it for me as back then you could use video recorders to record direct from the TV. This was another video that I nearly wore out. The live concert had scaffolding as the stage backdrop and while my stage was limited to the front room I would often use the plastic slide we had to create it. I would put my Cher records on and pretend to be the diva herself. I walked around a lot in the early days with a piece of hoover that I used as a microphone.

This whole set up was perfect and summer holidays tended to be perfect for being Cher. Mum would be busy in the kitchen keeping Hazel my sister happy, so I would pop a record on and depending what mood I felt in would become Cher, Donna Summer or Yazz. The only drawback with using the slide as a stage, was that it created a lot of static electricity. Every now and then it would create a shock or make a hiss or sometimes bit of a bang. No problem when one has an imagination like mine, these where merely pyrotechnics and part of the act.

I sometimes wonder if Mum brought out the gay man in me without meaning to. We had a dressing up box that was for me and Hazel. Mum would dump clothes, shoes and boots in it that she didn't want. One day in popped a pair of grey ankle boots, that was it, they were mine! They looked very similar to a pair that Cher had worn. I often think this was my early drag days. (you will discover more on this later).

As I got older, these artists stayed with me, but new additions came along. I became very aware of Meat Loaf and loved the more louder rock sound. I later went onto discover Alice Cooper and Dio. This was a big change for me. Alice Cooper took the idea of showmanship to an all-time new level. It was loud, dark, sinister with hint of evil, but also complete genius. He built this character that was a mix of all the dark elements, I had loved as a child watching the pantomime villains and it was all rolled into this one stage character.

Lots of his songs resonated with me on a deep level, when you strip them back and look at the story and what is being projected it is very powerful stuff. Schools Out for Summer is one of Alice Cooper's best-known songs – and the summer was also my favourite time of year. The holidays felt never-ending, and it was great that you get to forget about school and all the worries that can bring with it and just focus on friends and family.

We used to have a caravan on the front drive, the idea being that one day we would go off on holiday in it. Well... that never quite happened, it ended up just sitting there for quite a few years. This didn't bother me and Hazel as it become our den or place to hang out.

We lived in a street called Styles Close and most of the kids formed part of a closed circle or gang. The caravan often became our base and a place we could go in and feel safe. On occasions we had sleepovers in there, but these didn't always go down too well as we tended to be very loud, and the caravan walls were thin.

So often we would get shouted at by Mum and Dad to be quiet and mindful that people were sleeping. We weren't trying to be loud we were just excited for our sleepover. Now and then when playing on the drive, we would hear the whistling tones or singing voice from the neighbour next door. There aren't really enough words to describe this gentleman, so I feel he needs a chapter of his own ...

Halloween – Dressed Up as Alice Cooper Ready to Scare the Neighbours

Charlie Murphy

For me, Charlie Murphy was the best neighbour you could ever ask for. He was a TRUE gentleman, an earth angel and made an impression on all of us that knew him. When we were quite young, he lived with his wife Violet, I don't remember too much about her other than she was a biggish lady, with purple rinsed hair in tight curls. She was a nurse in her younger days but became ill with... well... we never really knew it was that was wrong with her, it always got referred to as 'woman's problems'.

From what Mum and Dad told me Charlie was a little bit henpecked by her, but she was his world and vice versa. She was a very well to do lady and didn't mince her words but once you got past her hard exterior her heart was in the right place. Before she passed, she was going in for surgery to have these 'woman's problems' sorted, she made Charlie promise to carry on and live life to the fullest if anything went wrong. She came around from the operation but died suddenly of a heart attack. Charlie's world was shattered yet he kept the promise he had made to her and did indeed live life to the fullest for his Violet, even though his heart was broken.

Often, we would be playing on the drive, or making teepees against the caravan with left over bamboo sticks from the garden that had been stored in the garage. Charlie would always come out and talk to us. He loved us like we were his grandchildren, and we viewed him as a grandfather figure. He always took an interest in what we were up to even though he probably didn't understand what we were on about half the time. Me and my sister had both quite active imaginations.

For me personally, I always felt he was sent from heaven to make up for the fact I didn't know very much about my Grampy on Mum's side. My Grampy, Robert Haskell, had become very ill and he was in a mental health institute. The only memory I have of him, was him handing me a bourbon biscuit and smiling when I had gone to visit him with my Dad. A few weeks later he tragically took his own life. I was far too young to understand what had gone on but that was the day my Mum's world was shattered.

I am often told stories of how much I take after my Grampy. Like me he was artistic and a creative, quiet at times and nervous. I often wonder what he would think of me now and the work I do. That was the first time I had seen the hurt and devastation that a suicide and a passing can bring to a person and a family. Interestingly, I get a lot of suicides coming through with my own mediumship work - it was explained by my mentor and others, because I have been through it myself on the receiving end. The spirit world trust and know I can deliver that type of information in a heartfelt and correct way. (My Grampy has come forward before in readings and on demo nights which is why I will not discuss his passing in too much detail. As its always a joy to hear from him and I am wary I would never want to feed a medium information.)

You usually would hear Charlie before you saw him. He had a lovely singing voice - I'm not sure he could sing exactly but it was still lovely and refreshing to hear. He would often sing or even have Tom Jones records blasting out whilst he pottered about in his garden. It was nice to hear someone still enjoying music at his age, we would often hear him belting out 'Delilah' or 'Green, Green Grass of Home'. When he wasn't singing, he would be whistling or even humming the tunes. Now... as a rule I hate whistlers, but this was different. Not a high pitch screech like my Dad makes, this was soulful and again in tune.

Charlie was a lover of charity shops, bric a brac, and car boot sales. Often he would come back on a Sunday morning with gifts or 'finds' as he called them. His favourite expression was 'too true' he tended to say it a lot at the end of a sentence. It always makes me smile when I hear someone else saying it in similar content. He tended to gift us very random and sometimes not always appropriate items for the age we were, much to my Mum's annoyance. It wasn't that we were ungrateful, but sometimes the stuff was just rubbish, jigsaw puzzles with main pieces missing, or books or colouring items without the crayons.

He did come up trumps one day and brought back an old-style double barrel gun. The thing was rusty, clearly some kind of antique and it made a loud bang sound when you pulled the trigger. I loved it, my sister loved it, but Mum was less than impressed. Me and my sister started to squabble over it and I think without being aware how heavy the thing was I knocked her on the head with it. That's it... the tears came out and I was in big trouble. Needless to say, I didn't see the gun again for quite a few years. A similar experience happened with a brolly that Charlie gave us, again my sister took the hit and got hurt and I received a good telling off and it got taken from us. I think Mum may have had a quiet word with Charlie as we didn't seem to get too many items after that.

From starting first school, right up until college days and after Charlie was always there in the background, never interfering but always there if you needed him. He would often ask how things were going, what we were studying etc., and he even met my partner Paul. I'm not sure if he quite grasped that we were a couple even though it was always made clear. I like to think it was never an issue as he never brought it up, he just accepted us both freely.

As time went on Charlie became ill, he had suffered a stroke and was starting to become forgetful. Suddenly it felt like the world was catching up with him. He was starting to look frail, and almost as though his once youthful looks had been robbed by Father Time. He would still greet us if we bumped into him but would often repeat himself, it was like you were having a conversation with a record that was scratched and kept going back to the start. He seemed at times very confused, he started mixing up who we were, and it was becoming clear the man we knew and loved was disappearing. Some years later he passed over to the spirit world. This was the first passing I had experienced that really hit home for me, I felt speechless. Tears were running down my face, but I wasn't sad. I was relieved he was at peace, I knew he would be looked after, I could sense and feel it in my heart.

I suddenly had an overwhelming smell of fresh mint around me. One of my memories of Charlie was he had mint plants growing everywhere in his garden. He invited me and Hazel round to see this plant and he talked to us about it. Rub the leaves and smell it the smell was strong, and sometimes overpowering.

The fact I was smelling this so strong and powerful for no reason, I knew it was a sign from him that he was home safe and with Violet once more.

Until we meet again thank you for being the person that loved us unconditionally. Never wanting or asking for anything in return, just being you was the greatest gift you could give us. The world became a little bit harder and more serious when we lost you my friend. I always feel he is up there with the other members of my family singing Delilah on a fluffy cloud watching over us all.

Charlie, Nan and Me

Christmas Magic

Christmas time was always exciting in the Garlington home - Mum went to town from us being at a young age to make it magical. I have never been religious, for me Christmas time was more about family and everyone celebrating the love together. When I was younger me and my sister used to get very excited for the presents. We were kids, that's what happens at that age!

Mum also loved Christmas so would decorate the place, and each year a different themed dressed tree would be created. Mum loved her tree to have the 'wow' factor and whatever the theme was, it delivered. Often being the talking point when friends and family came over. Some years it would be a posh artificial tree, other years they had a real one. You had to watch out for the pine needles with the real one as they got caught in your socks and that hurt if you hadn't noticed they were there.

Mum didn't just go to town with decorations, she wanted to make Christmas special and magical for us. She would often get friends and family to write our gift tags claiming they were from Santa! We wouldn't recognise the writing, so it must be Santa! It was also a big deal to leave a glass of wine out and some carrots for Rudolph and some Quality Street chocolates for Santa! No mince pies from us though, apparently Santa wasn't keen on those Dad said with a smile.

The aim with Christmas was to go to bed early so Santa could deliver the goods! This seemed to be the longest night's sleep ever. I would look at the clock and it would be like time was going backwards. Me and my sister were so excited that we couldn't sleep, I wanted to catch a glimpse of this Santa once and for all! There was always a present from him in my room of a morning. I decided I was indeed going to stay awake and catch him, I never did but always seemed to have a habit of waking up early.

4.00 am — Hmm a bit early I'll nip to the loo and see what's happening - the house was still and silent. Back to bed for a bit.

4.30 am — Hmm still too early.

5.00 am — The present that Santa has left was on my desk. Would I be allowed to open this yet? I slowly started to tear open the paper as quietly as possible as to not make a noise. The latest Lego set, yet again he delivered the goods, he always seemed to know what I wanted.

5.30 am — Hmm I wonder if Hazel is up? I would sneak into her room and have a look see. Sometimes she was awake sometimes she pretended to be asleep, hmm best give her a poke, would hate for her to miss out on the presents. We usually ended up camping on her bed and whispering away about the magic Christmas brings with it.

6.00 am — Hmm I think that's late enough. We both snuck downstairs and turned on the lights. Most times Mum would already be down there making a tea in the dark, or we would wake her up en route and she would come down. Whilst she wasn't keen on the early rises, she did enjoy seeing us opening the gifts, and our little faces lighting up.

Dad on the other hand was a bit more annoying! He didn't get up early, more like 8.00 am or 9.00 am depending on how he was feeling. He was then so slow to open anything. We wanted to see what he had got so we would often pile up the presents around his seat. I swear it made him go extra slow. Even now he will not be rushed and will sometimes do a present an hour!

These memories are such happy times for me. It's only when you look back that I realise Mum and Dad really did go all out and put a lot of effort in. Thank you from the bottom of my heart to them for making Christmas a magical family time.

Getting Hyper at Witchy Gifts on Christmas Day

A Doorway to Another Realm

It must have been when I was around the age of ten or eleven, the year 1996. This was my first encounter with something other worldly. I have always believed in other realms and worlds that collide and exist within our own. I feel there are portals and doorways to other realms it's just knowing where they are. One of my favourite films growing up was Willow, whilst this is based on a fantasy idea, I think there is a lot of truth to parts of the story. This is my own belief, and everyone is entitled to believe what they feel sits right for them.

People laugh when I tell them about this, and look at me as if to say 'Really?' but this was something that I can remember so vividly and have never been able to explain, even now it bothers me that I cannot fully understand what I witnessed. I think when you open up to the bigger world around you, it really changes the way you view things. I have often learnt that things I thought were impossible can actually be reality.

We had done the morning traditions on this Christmas Day, one thing that happened was every other year we would have my Nan (Mum's Mum) to stay for lunch. She lived in Bathampton so whilst Mum would be preparing the Christmas Roast dinner me and Dad (occasionally Hazel but usually me and Dad) would go and pick up my Nan.

Outside our house on the drive we had two massive Conifer trees, one either side. When we were smaller these were a frequent hiding place as they were literally so big, you could crawl inside them and hide. The one nearest to the door had less branches on the bottom. I think where they had grown so big and people kept brushing past them, they had snapped off, so you could clearly see the base part of the tree and the roots. They looked lovely but smelt horrible.

This particular morning, we had to go and collect Nan. Dad was busy getting ready, so I went on out to the car. Whilst going outside I stopped dead in my tracks, the front door still partially open. What I can only describe as a little woodland gnome, or dwarf was standing in front of me. He was wearing green and brown clothing, a little pointy hat, and had a look of autumn about him. A small dirty face and beady little eyes looking at me. He didn't say a word but started to run around the tree.

A mix of feelings came over me, at first, I thought had Santa left behind one of his helpers. Even though I was aware at this age that Mum and Dad were Santa! I next thought, is this a kid messing around or having a 'wind up' or has Mum set someone up?

I continued to watch as this little man danced around the tree. By this time Dad had started coming out of the front door. The little man ran into the hidey hole within the tree, I immediately followed, once inside there was only one way back out. As I followed him, he literally vanished, I would love to be able to say that I saw a little door open within the tree, sadly I did not. But the little man had completely disappeared, there was nowhere he could have gone once he was inside. I didn't understand what I had just witnessed and felt confused and frustrated. My Dad started calling me and began asking what I was doing in the tree? I explained to him, being Dad, he was less than impressed. "Come on, we will be late collecting your Nan" was the reply.

Before we left, I ran back inside and demanded to know from Mum what game she had set up. She looked at me confused as she stood over the sink peeling the potatoes. Me and Mum have always been very in tune with each other. We can give each other a look and know exactly what the other person is thinking, almost like a conversation telepathically. I could see by her reaction that she genuinely had no idea what I was on about. But she could also see from my reaction that something had clearly spooked me, and I wasn't making anything up.

With Dad getting impatient to get going I had no choice but to admit defeat. I checked around the tree once more before I got on in the car. No sign of a little hat being left or any other clues as to what I had witnessed. I didn't talk too much about it to my Dad on the journey down, as he wasn't interested in that kind of conversation.

When we collected my Nan, I did mention it to her. She was a bit of a character my Nan, although lots of family members struggled with her. She wasn't always the easiest person to get along with – Mum had a bit of a love/hate relationship with her. But regardless of this Mum always did her utmost for her right until the day she died, and I know she loved her unconditional in her own way. Nan just smiled at me, she also loved anything fantasy related and was big into fairies. "If you saw a little man, Gnome, or Dwarf, then that's what you saw" was her reply. Simple and to the point, that's what I loved about her she would always say it as it was. Like me, I don't think she needed to be convinced but she was very private with what she believed in, looking back now I feel she was a lot more spiritual and gifted than she let on.

So, was that it – this little creature from another land or world, shows itself to me and keeps me guessing? I've been guessing ever since! Every day for about a year or so after I would check both trees pretty much daily, but never saw or witnessed anything like that again. It was strange as I had always had a bit of a soft spot for the trees, and a kind of feeling of respect. Dad and Mum would often moan about how big and unsightly they were becoming. I often saw them more as protectors of the family home we lived in, eventually years later they got cut down. I often wonder if that was a portal or doorway to another world and had I been chosen to potentially witness? So many questions that would never get answered.

One thing I do know is that the experience I had witnessed was indeed 100% real and seemed to be for my eyes only. I have spoken about this in later years to spiritual and witchy friends and those that work with the fairy realms. Lots of them too have had similar experiences when they were younger, and some when they have been older. I guess if those mystical creatures choose to find you and work with your energy for whatever reason they may have they will find you at any age, as and when they feel ready. As soon as you go looking for them you very rarely find them. One thing I have learned from being a Medium, both the spiritual world and other realms work on their terms.

Little Fairy Door Seen on a Trip to Cornwall (What I Wanted to See in the Tree on my Drive)

Popular.... Or Not

Whilst I loved my primary and first school, middle school was a different ball game! This was at a stage of my journey where I felt things where becoming a little bit darker. First school was amazing we were at the highest-class year, so we were considered the big kids in the school. People looked up to us as the ones that had survived, and we had the power. Middle school was tricky though. The safety net that had been build up around us was taken away. We found ourselves in the first year again, so naturally the year that all the other kids gave abuse out to.

Even harder for me, Kirsty's parents decided to move away to Holland and my main friend had been taken away from me! We promised to keep in touch and she had explained it was only for a few years with her Dad's work and they would be returning. Foolishly at that age we thought we would be able to sustain the friendship we had created – the reality was that didn't happen, and we didn't hear from each other for a long time.

Middle school was a bag of emotions both up and down. A mix of teaching, mental abuse and testosterone. It was becoming clearer that I was in touch with my feminine side, I seemed to gravitate towards the female energies. The first couple of years were bearable I would get the odd remark here and there but nothing major.

I was however starting to become quite quiet and shy. In my last school I was pretty chatty and outgoing. I felt as though people around me didn't really want to hear what I had to say so I wouldn't speak unless I needed to. Whilst the girls were happy for me to hang around with them in the early days as time went on, I was cramping their style. They were starting to become interested in boys and the attention that they craved went with it. I suddenly found myself on the outside of a circle looking in. I didn't really have anyone around me that I could call a friend. My sister started the middle school as I moved up a year, this became helpful for me as we would walk to and from school together. I loved my sister dearly and she was and still is one of my best friends, I think she managed to survive a little better than me, although she says she had it just as tough.

Lunch breaks were filled with wandering around the playground alone and praying that I could just get on and be me without having any abuse or stupid comments thrown my way. I would often wish for the bell to ring earlier, so we could at least get through to the lessons. People didn't seem to be quite as harsh when I was in a lesson.

As time went on, I was embraced into a different circle of people. Not the typical girls I had been around before. This was a group of guys, they were slightly alternative, and definitively free spirited. Whilst I was still very quiet, they took me in and I was able to roam around with them. They didn't seem to care too much if I spoke or not. But if someone talked bad of me, they would defend me. I kind of become their property or that's how it felt, it was all a bit weird, but it was better than circling the playground for an hour alone.

The group of lads was a bit of mismatch of people, we were seven in total. There was one really good-looking guy that all the girls wanted as their boyfriend the rest had longer hair, smoked weed at the top end of the field, and weren't really interested in the lessons, they were just happy plodding about their day. Then there was me who was taking everything in but was only really speaking as and when I needed to. Whilst some of them did drugs, it was never something they made me do, it was offered I refused and that was that. They got on and did it, I just watched with the non-drug takers in the group. One of them had carved a big hole in the earth and pulled up half the grass, they then inserted a tin deep within. This was their stash as they called it, which housed different forms of substances for when they needed a fix. There were others in our year that did different forms of drugs, but they would often get caught by the 'dinner dogs' (or lunchtime supervisors I believe is the correct title).

Whilst the guys I hung around with looked as thick as two short planks, they were pretty switched on and made sure they covered all their tracks. They were the only group of people that never got caught despite the fact they stunk of whatever they had been smoking or inhaling. Polo mints and Lynx body spray plastered on as lunch came to an end before afternoon classes would resume. I often wondered how they got through the afternoon classes, they were all high as a kite, but they seemed to plod along regardless.

One time and one time only, one of the group decided to do some poppers before they had to endure the torture that was maths. Once again, I was offered but for some reason still unknown to me now, I thought 'sod it, why not, what's the worst that can happen' and gave in. A small black bottle with white lid was presented towards me. It smelt like a mix of Vicks Vapour Rub mixed with vodka and Red Bull. "What is this?" I asked. "Never mind what's in it just take a deep sniff on it". I did as I was instructed, I felt as if I had burned all my nose hair as I inhaled this mixture deep in.

Within minutes my head began to pulsate and spin. "How do you feel?" one of them asked. I felt as if the room was spinning and I was stuck on a waltzer ride that was on repeat. "Are you buzzing?" someone asked. I had never felt so ill in all my life. As I stumbled into maths the teacher took one look at me and said: "Michael are you OK, you don't look so good". "I feel a bit sick..." as soon as I said it, that was it, projectile vomit everywhere! I was sent to the Nurses' office which was a little room within the school library. A mix of burned out souls trying to get out of PE were already there. They took a look at me and could see that I wasn't quite at my best! My face had become white and I was talking nonsense. In the end Mum had to be called in to escort me home.

I was able to blame the school dinners this time, and she never knew what had occurred. Needless to say, I never touched any of the stuff again. Why on earth would people pay stupid amounts of money to feel that way? I just did not get it and still don't to this day. Your self-worth must be rock bottom to go through that kind of pain and torture. To me it felt horrible, I just didn't understand or get the buzz I was meant to feel. Had I done it wrong? Was there some after affect I was going to experience? No, that was your lot!

It made me more anti-drug than I had been before. Looking back now I'm glad it was only poppers I tried as if I had tried some hardcore drug, I question if I would have survived the experience. People must be in so much hurt and pain to feel that they need this junk to switch the world off for a while. Whereas I felt blessed for the life I had, regardless of how lonely it felt. What on earth were the guys around me thinking or going through?

The Lost Boy – I Can See the Sadness in My Eyes

The Invisible Teacher

Maths class seemed to be when all the weird stuff occurred, I guess because it bored the hell out of me my mind would go wandering. The teacher was a small petite lady called Mrs Shaw. She had big round eyes that seemed to burn deep into your soul which would make it uncomfortable to look at her for too long. She also had an unusual haircut - it wasn't so much that it was unusual, you just questioned if it was her real hair. Imagine those people that have a bowl placed on their head and harshly cut around it to form a 'perfect bob' – well that was her. Also, it was ginger with red dyed strands going through and grey highlights. Clearly a bottle job that had not been done very well! People often questioned if this 'nest' on her head was real. Sometimes it did seem to appear a tad wonky on her head, or the fringe would be too far forward. Personally, I feel it was her own hair - just badly maintained.

    One lesson she decided we were going to learn about pie and square, this literally went over my head! As she started conducting the lesson, I noticed there was an older taller gentleman next to her. He was tall but slender dressed in a casual grey suit. He had brown eyes with white hair and a little bit of a beard but not fully grown. He was sitting comfortably in a chair looking around and watching over everyone.

'How rude' I thought, that she was muttering away and had forgotten to introduce this other teacher that I presumed wanted to stand in on the lesson. All whilst she was busy getting all excited and started writing what could have been Egyptian hieroglyphics on the whiteboard, that no one in the room had any clue what she was going on about!

I asked the person sitting next to me "Who is that man? he has not been introduced." This seemed most out of character, Mrs Shaw was a very friendly and forthcoming teacher, it just seemed so odd she had cut him dead and had not acknowledged his presence. The person sitting next to me gave me a look of disgust! "What are you on about, there is no man there." I was shocked, was this another one that had been joining my gang at the top of the field? He is right in front of us looking and listening. I asked the person on the opposite side of me for more of a rational explanation. "Who is that male teacher she has forgot to introduce to the class?" Again, a look of disgust was thrown my way. "What are you on about, there is no one there only Mrs Shaw."

Goosebumps suddenly filled my arms and legs, I continued to study this gentleman. I saw him plain as day and as clear as anyone else in the room, yet for some unknown reason the two idiots either side of me could not or did not want to see him. I was confused, watched on as he looked my way and smiled.

This was ridiculous, I wanted answers! I put my hand up to ask who he was, and Mrs Shaw smiled and asked if I had a question about pie. Suddenly the man sitting next to her vanished - completely gone! My hand fell and I remained silent. What had I just witnessed? This wasn't seconds or a split minute, this gentleman was clear in my mind. I could see how he looked and describe what he was wearing. Where did he go? Did Mrs Shaw have a trap door in the floor I hadn't known about? I started asking others in the class had anyone seen the gentleman teacher, they all looked at me as if I was crazy. No one in the room had seen him apart from me. I felt a mix of emotions - anger, frustration, but also excitement. What had I just experienced?...

Looking back, I now realise that spirit wanted to work with me even back then. But I was not ready to fully embrace them. They gave me a small slice of the cake to whet my appetite and that was enough to keep me guessing for several years. I now feel this gentleman was either a spirit guide, or my Grandad. I will never fully know. I now view them as a doorkeeper that was watching over me in my hour of need.

I noticed there seemed to be a pattern forming. When I felt stressed or highly-strung weird stuff tended to happen more. Sometimes as I was loathing the riddle Mrs Shaw was writing on the white board I would see colours around her - sometimes greens, other times reds or blues. But there was always something depending on how her mood was that day.

Middle school was harder for me, and I was stressed a lot of the time. I used to ask in my head and send my thoughts - not to God but to my Grandad or whoever was in charge and pulling the strings up there. Whenever I asked for help, I seemed to receive it, not always in the way I would have expected but... it always came to me one way or another.

I went through a stage of walking home on my own from school. My sister had started walking home with a group of her friends, she had become a bit of a social butterfly by then and I was happy for her. There were some kids down the street that did not mix well with the rest of us. They came across as complete bullies and were just that! I didn't understand their view on the world, they were loud and vile, they only seemed happy when putting others down.

The aim when walking home alone was to get out of class as quickly as possible and power walk. I got to the lollypop lady that stopped the traffic, so you could safely cross the road. On down to the little alley that went around the back of the park - so far so good. Past the Spar shop on the corner, I was doing well no sign of anyone I would be back home in no time.

Halfway down the hill I stopped dead in my tracks. There was the gang that for whatever reason that I am still unaware of to this day made my life awkward – no, unbearable! I could handle being bullied, but this just seemed to be every day! There was no let up and I was becoming drained and tired. As soon as they clocked you were behind them, they started to walk slower. Great! I had a few options - either I slowed down too although I would have to go snail's pace to get home. I could take my chances and go around them, or I could go down a side road that would add another twenty minutes to the journey and make Mum, who would be waiting for me and knew roughly what time I usually came in, angry with panic. We didn't have mobile phones back then, so unless there was a payphone close by it was hard to contact her to say I would be late.

I decided taking a power walk and overtaking the idiots was my best option. As I started walking up the hill, I asked my Grandad in my head 'please keep me safe and no harm to come to me'. I wasn't keen on fighting and had seen these guys had all been in fights before.

I continued up the hill and started to overtake, one of them tried to trip me up but missed. A second one tried and did make me lose balance briefly. I prayed in my head for my Grandad to keep me safe. Whilst I never saw this personally or thought maybe I did have a mince to my walk, they would often shout out "Skippy!" and start singing Skippy the Bush Kangaroo at me. I turned up the little row of steps and power walked the last stretch. As soon as my feet hit the drive, I felt I was on home turf and safe. I thanked my Grandad for me not getting beaten up and went inside as if nothing had happened.

That's how it tended to be three days out of five, occasionally if I got out early enough, I would have a clear run and a quiet walk home. I cherished those rare days, the rest of the time I felt like I had to have eyes and ears everywhere.

I often look back at this and whilst I feel it was hard and unnecessary, I thank my spirit guides, door keeps, angels and my Grandad for watching over me. I always felt when I asked for help it was given to me and felt like it would all be ok. They wouldn't allow any harm or hurt to come my way. I managed to just about survive so for this I feel eternally grateful. I feel blessed to say that I have never been involved in a hands-on fight, I hope I never have to experience this.

For me violence has never resolved anything, and I don't understand the 'cave man' approach that people have around it. I know there were other people in my year who were bullied. Some was from mental abuse, some was physical, both where unnecessary. I love the fact that nowadays more holistic avenues are being introduced into schools for example mindfulness and meditation. If we had that back then who knows, things may have been different?

I will never understand why someone feels they have to dominate, control, or put another person down. They may feel they are big, hard or clever, but the reality and truth of the matter is they just show the world the ugliest side they have within them. A deep underlining issue, or emotional garbage that they need to explore and make peace with. I hope in time children can grow and learn in a place of love and peace. I welcome this new world with open arms.

Empty Chairs, Empty Stares

Phases

Outside of school I would go through phases of things I would want to pursue. Some were a little more achievable than others! When I was young, I decided guitar lessons was the way forward. My Mum and Dad bought me a beautiful acoustic guitar. It was lovely, it came in its own carrying case and the smell of new leather was strong. We searched and found a teacher that offered private lessons after school, perfect! I was booked in and off I went - well... for whatever reason still unknown to me, this gentleman (I can't remember his name) took a bit of a dislike to me.

I had just sat in the chair and it was as if I was in trouble. He had a very low tolerance and didn't seem to like it if you misplaced your fingers on the strings. After about three lessons that was it, he was doing my head in. The idea of learning the guitar suddenly did not interest me. I was finding at times I was becoming quite psychic and picking up on peoples' feelings, energies and emotions. At this point whilst I was young, this gentleman was so negative, and I was feeling drained. All the fun and excitement I had about wanting to learn the guitar, he had crushed very early on and ruined for me. Years later, I found out he suffered with extreme bipolar, and had issues with alcohol, that was probably why I felt so drained around him, I had been tapping into his energy and not liking it without being aware what was happening.

A few years went by and I started watching the TV series 'The Masked Magician', that was it, I was hooked. The TV series was a bit of a taboo back then. Some well-known magician who was in the magic circle decided to leak how big stage illusions and smaller ones were done. The magic was not so impressive once you had learnt how it was achieved. Regardless of this, it became my new bug and I started investing in good quality magic sets and tricks. No half measures with me, I wanted to order blades to use but due to my age being under 18 it was a no go. Probably for the best, as my poor sister became my assistant. I used to nag her could she do it with me.

One time when I was really into my magic, I decided we should put on a show for the other kids in the street. I made a few stage tricks out of old cardboard boxes and other bits of crap. Bamboo canes became just as good as swords. My poor sister would be placed in this rather large cardboard box, whilst I had made pre-made holes that you couldn't see from looking at it and would shoot these sticks in with some speed without hitting her (well, that was the plan). A couple of times she did get hurt in rehearsals, but it always went OK on the night. We had a large collection of music between us, and the deal was she got to pick the tapes we used for background music.

On reflection, not the best idea having Aqua's – 'Barbie Girl' when you're performing an illusion! Regardless of this we got through the show and it was fairly good, I think. After a while magic began to bore me, it seemed there was a lot more hours you had to put in before you became good at it. I wasn't lazy, but I was impatient and wanted instant results. So slowly the magic stopped, and the once beloved tricks and sets were put in the loft to gather dust.

Music had always played a big role with me in one form or another. I decided I would like to learn the piano or keyboard as it ended up being. Mum and Dad were very skeptical of this decision. They asked me about eight or nine times if I was sure, 'yes' I really felt like this was my way forward in life. We went to a little music shop at the top of Frome that offered lessons and met with the teacher.

Weirdly there was a few familiar faces in the class. One of the druggy gang - I didn't know he went and played keyboard, and it was clearly a shock for me to see him there. Regardless I felt even more sure this could only be a good thing. The lessons were a little different there, you had to sign up to a block of classes for two months at a time. Mum and Dad booked the two months and off we went.

They refused to buy a keyboard for me to practice on however due to the whole guitar business. It all started off well and I was getting the hang of it. Occasionally I would get my left and rights mixed up but usually tumbled through. It was clear after two months that if I was to get anywhere with this, I would need a keyboard to practice on. Reluctantly my Dad bought me an ex-display keyboard they were getting rid of in the music shop. This was the business! For its time it was high spec, I was made up and set it up in my room.

Now I had the new keyboard I must commit and practice regularly in between lessons. "Yes, yes" I said, 'stop pestering me' I felt. I bought a load of show tune music books, I was getting very into my musicals by then and I had discovered the magic of Andrew Lloyd Webber. While everyone was on blue book level 1 playing Three Blind Mice, I decided I would learn a few songs from Joseph and his Technicolour Dream Coat. Sometimes I would get it and it would flow well, other times it sounded like random keys being smacked around.

On occasion my Nan would spend the day with us, these rare times I would perform the show tunes for her. I think she was less than impressed but she humoured me. Part of the course involved going to Birmingham to watch a keyboard concert. It was attended by a collection of everyone else that the music shop had helped to show how far they had come. My Nan went with me and it was a magical day. I can't remember all of it now, but it was one of my favourite memories of my Nan. We definitively got to learn a little more about each other that day and agreed that what went on in Birmingham stayed in Birmingham!

As time went on boredom reared its head once more. I stuck with the keyboard for about a year and a half. But then it started to constrict me, I found it was starting to become very technical. The fun easy-going approach had gone, and certificates were starting to be talked about and tests done to get to the following stages. The free spirit of music making was no more. I knew if I wanted to progress, I would need to complete these tests and qualifications. The problem I had was, I felt yet again I was being hurried along. Why was everyone so worried about achieving this before a certain date? It's like time wasn't on their side.

I personally felt in no great hurry, I was happy to just plod along and enjoy the music making for what it was. Others in the group took it all very seriously, some have even gone onto become professional musicians. I guess for me I didn't share the passion in quite the same way. I enjoyed more the experience rather than the pressure people wanted to put on me.

I decided that the music had to stop and left the class. Mum and Dad were less than impressed. Even though I felt I had done well sticking it out for that time, they felt a bit let down, and yet again money had been wasted! I kept the keyboard for quite a few years after and now and then had a little play about on it, but it didn't feel the same, the magic it once created was definitively gone.

Outside of school, things where pretty good. The average evening depending on what day it fell on, would consist of homework, then dinner, and then me and my sister going to hang around with the other kids in the street. Part of our gang was made up of two Catholic girls that lived down the bottom end of the road, Jennifer and Deborah. Whilst they went to a Catholic school and we only saw them outside of school time they became our best friends, and we formed 'the fabulous four'.

Jennifer and I were the older ones within the group and as we got older, hormones started to kick in, and puberty started to surge through us all. It was a weird time for me, I knew in my heart I was gay, but it's like I was waiting to deal with it. Looking back now I knew I was gay probably from around the age of six or seven. It's hard to explain, I didn't fancy boys at that age but when I would look through Mum's weekly magazines, they would sometimes have a picture of a hunky bloke in there. I always seemed to stop and feel more drawn towards them. It was like I wanted to study them more than the glamorous females within the magazine or on the telly in certain programmes. I knew that at some point I would need to tackle this, I also knew that this was going to be a big taboo for people within the family and probably the hardest thing I would have to face.

For reasons I still can't quite remember now, me and Jennifer ended up being a couple. This all felt a bit weird and very unnatural. Yet part of me liked the attention it brought with it. I think we did love each other as friends and cared a lot for each other, but we definitely were not in love - I certainly wasn't. I think we both felt a little confused and it seemed the right thing to do, for everyone else outside looking in. It almost felt like everyone else saw us as a couple, so we kind of gave it a try. It was doomed from the start, and another phase that would be short lived...

Awakening to the Spirit Within

I'm Coming Out

Mine and Jennifer's relationship felt odd and wrong in some many ways. We lasted in total about fourteen months. In that time, we went through the good, the bad, and the ugly. Everything started out being lovely, but it was clear its days were numbered. We got together when I was in the last year of middle school and we went into college. College for me was like the fire pit of hell, whilst there I didn't speak unless I had to. The only saving grace was Jennifer went to a different college, so she never knew how I was. If she had seen me there, she probably wouldn't have wanted to associate with me.

I was definitely the odd ball, the weird kid, the outsider. Whilst it had been OK and a little cool at St John's, there was nothing cool about it now. My world felt very lonely, my emotions felt all over the place. My psychic side had truly switched itself on and I seemed unsure how to turn this off. When I was around certain teachers or students it was like I could feel all their emotions. I became so empathic but again had been unaware of what was happening.

Me and Jennifer plodded along as best we could. We did kiss each other but we didn't always feel we could do it in public. There was an old train bridge nearby, so we would often go for walks and chats and end up there. That's where we used to make out. It was pretty overgrown and hardly anyone used it, so it seemed the perfect spot.

We would have a bit of a snog and cuddle (that's as far as it went on the bridge). It always felt an odd sensation, I quite enjoyed the cuddle and embrace of feeling loved. The snogging was a different matter Jennifer at the time had braces, so there was the added pressure of not getting your tongue or gums sliced open! I was also very particular so didn't always feel I could kiss her when we had been eating certain foods.

The months plodded along, and she started to want to take things to the next level. I guess that's what happens in a relationship. She started inviting me around the house when both her parents and sister were out. We would meet up and just chat, again more snogging. As we carried on it was clear more demands were being expected of me. The problem was I didn't feel I could deliver the goods. I sometimes questioned if I was bisexual, I would go through and rattle it all away in my head.

There was a guy in the same year at college who hung around with the druggy gang I was still in and out of. His name was Karl and he was drop dead gorgeous, he was a complete idiot though, not so much with myself but just in general. I definitely fancied him, the feeling was very strong inside. I always felt he had a little soft spot for me, he always seemed to act nice around me. He probably could see how much crap I took from others so felt sorry for me, but he did seem to have a bit of respect that was very welcomed. Whilst he was not gay, I feel he may have dabbled if the offer came his way, it never did so I will never know. The feelings I had for him were strong, not like what I was experiencing with Jennifer.

I decided I was getting in way over my head and needed to shut this down with Jennifer ASAP before someone got hurt badly. Before I could say anything, she wanted to meet up with me. She sounded pretty angry on the phone. One thing I had learnt from being in a relationship with her, was that females seemed to blow very hot and cold for no real reason. I never seemed to know when I was in the doghouse and for what reason. She sat me down and wanted to know why I didn't want to have sex with her! Whilst we were in a relationship, we were both still quite young, I'm not sure I would have been ready for any sexual relationship. (Possibly if Karl had knocked on my door, I may have made an exception!)

I felt as if I was being suffocated, she was starting to make me feel uncomfortable and as if I needed to justify my reasons why. I tried to brush it off the first time and said I didn't feel ready. She was having none of it! I felt gosh this is all getting a bit awkward and a bit much.

I decided the time was now, I could no longer go on patching up the holes, the cracks in the relationship were starting to get too big. There wasn't going to be a good time to drop the bombshell, so I figured a bit like a plaster I just had to rip it off quickly. I sat her down and explained that I did love her, but I wasn't sure I was in love with her. I told her I thought I was gay, and how I had these feelings for some time. I closed my eyes and waited for a hard slap around my face. Instead I was shocked she ended up being at the time very supportive and threw her arms around me. I felt like the weight of the world had been lifted! I had told someone, and it was official, it felt comfortable and correct.

Jennifer put on a brave face, but I knew I had broken her heart. A few days later we met up and she seemed a little odd around me. She kept asking too many questions on the subject for my liking. 'Are you sure?' 'Have you even been with a man?' 'How do you know?' It took a lot for me to open up and tell her what was happening, so I didn't need her questioning everything. She explained to me she thought one day we might get married have children and be a family. I had just gone through puberty and that was definitely not on my wavelength in the foreseeable future. I decided I needed to act quickly, I didn't want her feeling like she had power over me! Whilst she was happy to keep it a secret for now, I knew that would be short lived and bitterness and anger was building up from inside her.

Next on the list was my sister, I thought she would be the easiest of the three immediate family to deal with. I sat her down and explained it all and told her - as expected she wasn't shocked. She said she had always known, and it didn't matter. Phew... it felt good having her know and be on my side - after all she was my bestie. She said she was a bit pissed off that Jennifer knew before her but could understand why. She loved me unconditionally and for that I am entirely grateful.

Then came Mum and Dad... gosh this was going to be hard. Dad has always had a very low tolerance level for things he doesn't understand. He often would mock and shout abuse to gay celebrities on the telly. This was part of the reason I never felt I could be completely myself with him, he made his feelings very clear. Growing up with my creative ways he would often say "are you a fag or sissy boy?". 'Be careful what you wish for Dad...' I used to think. I don't think he is a homophobic person he just doesn't understand it. For him, mocking something he can't get his head around is easier than acknowledgment.

I sat Mum down but for some reason the words just would not flow. "What is it son?" she would say "you know you can tell me anything". I knew I could, yet the words just would not come up. It took me several attempts and then she finally said, "are you gay?" That's a bit direct I thought. I suddenly had a feeling that my sister had told her, on this occasion I was glad, "Yes I think I am". Like my sister, she was disappointed I couldn't come to her first, but what doesn't kill you makes you stronger. We became closer afterwards, all the skeletons were out of the closet. There was just one more person I had to deal with. Mum didn't want me to tell Dad straightaway. Everyone was fearful of how he would react, so the next few months were spent trying to soften the blow...

Me and Paul in the Early Days

Distraction – Strike a Pose.....

If I thought middle school was bad, college took that to a whole new level. I started to feel like I had depression, it felt like it was more than just a teenage mood swing. My thoughts seemed to go very high and very low within seconds. Hate and vile abuse seemed to be spat at me everywhere, but I had become tired and immune to the negativity around me. I had no energy left to stand up and fight back so I literally let it wash over my head. What the bullies failed to understand was, I really was past caring. The aim was to survive the last few months of college for which you had to do by law, then you had the choice if you wanted to stay on to do A levels or leave and get a job in the real world.

I feel in the last stages of my college days art and photography really saved me. I think if I hadn't had these to chuck myself into my creative side, I would have taken my own life at this point in my journey. Often, I would go and walk on the train bridge that once housed mine and Jennifer's romance, I would spend time up there and ponder and think about life. Occasionally I would climb up onto the ledge of the train bridge, so it felt like I was suspended over the edge. Sometimes a train would randomly appear from nowhere, catching me off guard and causing the whole bridge to shake and vibrate, so I had to hold on tight as not to fall to my death.

Once or twice when I felt at my lowest, I did wonder 'would anyone notice if I just quietly let go and slip away?' But remembering the hurt and pain that my Grandads passing caused I couldn't and wouldn't put my family through that.

What I loved about both photography and art was that there were no limitations, nothing was off limits. I really enjoyed both my teachers for these subjects, they had a thirst for life and creative ideas, the wackier and more unusual the more they would encourage and try to bring it out of you. The photography classroom was spilt into two sections, with the actual classroom part, and through a corridor into a large laboratory that was 'The Dark Room'. This was pitch black with infra-red light. As you walked in, there was a work station in the middle full of all different trays. It stunk of chemicals this was the room where you could develop and print films you had taken yourself.

The art section of the college was built in one of the older parts of the building and it felt alive with spiritual activity. In both photography and art weird stuff would often happen. I was at the time becoming very clairaudient - I was starting to hear voices. I couldn't really make out what was being said but I could clearly hear whisperings. I always felt as if older teachers from before looked after that whole part of the building and watched on the students of this time. There was an air of mystic about it and it literally became my second home.

What was great about this was that the teachers encouraged you to work in there during your lunch break. Both subjects where quite intense so the more time you could dedicate the better. I think this is probably why I did well in both these subjects. I was left alone, and I could tap into my creative energy and it was celebrated, I decided to spend as much time in there as I could. Gone were the days of having to roam the playground like a loser or drift around with the druggy squad. There would always be a mixed bag of people at lunch time a few that would always be there like myself trying to escape the outside world, and then others that would come and go.

The dark room was a weird place. When it was busy with a class full of people it felt very safe and cosy, but when you were the only one in it or there was only the odd few, it had a very cold creepy atmosphere. People often said it was haunted and weird stuff had been reported. One day I was in there minding my own business the teacher was out front on lunch break marking some books, I was in there alone trying to get a reel of film undone and onto the developing reel. (It was important no light hit it otherwise your film and what was on it would be gone forever!)

I suddenly heard footsteps behind me, 'hmm a little odd' I thought to myself perhaps my teacher had come in. I looked over my shoulder but no one there, this happened three or four times, but I was determined to get on with the task in hand. I then used one of the enlargers to put the image onto photographic paper. Next, I took this over to the developing trays to start to print my photos, as I was at the first tray I felt something brush my leg. I looked down and next to me was a pair of feet and the start of some legs. This did make me jump I have to say, but I didn't run out screaming. This had become a sacred space for me, so I wasn't about to give it up. I stood my ground and made it clear to this spirit gentleman that I could see him, I was causing no harm and would respect the place. After that, everything seemed fine and the atmosphere felt calm and cosy once more.

Another time, I heard a gaggle of people gossiping, it almost felt as if they were talking about me. I heard one or two words but not much of the conversation, the voices sounded female. I did hear someone say "he is ok, he can stay" so, I'm guessing I wasn't a threat to anyone.

During my time studying photography and art, many weird things did happen. Equipment would often end up going from one side of the room to the other and I was starting to see a lot of smoky build-up of people, I almost started going into trance like states at times. Looking back this was a bit weird as it is the very same environment that trance mediumship is done in. Infra-red light is used when you do trance mediumship and go in a cabinet. Yet again, spirit were making it known to me that they wanted to work. But I did not feel ready, so pushed and blocked that side and closed off as best I could for many years.

It could be hard to get the right exposures for the prints, too quick and they would come out light like a ghost when developed. If over exposed, they would just go pitch black. I found when I was developing my prints in the tray, before the actual image started coming through, I would see random faces or images shown to me in the tray. I later discovered this to be another form of mediumship, water scrying. Spirits can show and manifest with great ease in water this way. I would often see faces that I didn't recognise before my actual print would start to appear.

My Dad could see that photography gave me part of my life back. Whilst I wasn't entirely happy as he still didn't know I was gay, it seemed to be a subject for the time being he didn't need to know about! I didn't feel great about keeping it from him, and I felt like I was walking on eggshells and borrowed time.

He turned part of the attic into my own darkroom. It was smaller than I was used to but had everything I needed. The great thing with this was I could get work done at evenings and weekends, my cousin had been big into photography and gave me some second-hand darkroom equipment. It wasn't brilliant but did the job and saved us a small fortune. I don't think my Dad ever realised just how grateful I am that he did that for me. It was a huge deal turning part of their home into a work space for me. I was and will always be eternally grateful - it's one of the best gifts he ever gave me.

I decided I wanted to be a Theatre photographer, this was a little bit looked down upon by my teacher at the time. It's a very overcrowded business and a lot of theatre companies have their own in-house photographers. I felt a little surprised and let down, I thought she would have been a bit more supportive! She was advising me down a safer kiddies or wedding photographer route - that did not interest me at all, I have never been one for kids! I ignored her suggestions and carried on with my long-term goal. I felt like I had done all this work for what, to become a children's photographer in some crappy studio! No, I don't think so, I wanted a new adventure... and a taste for the bigger world, I knew I had scratched the surface and there was more to come from life.

Working the Camera

The One Night Stand That Didn't Leave ...

I haven't talked to much so far about the relationship with my partner Paul. He is a very private person and our relationship is overall quite private in general. Whilst some people broadcast their every move to the world, we are and have always been a little more discrete.

Paul was a van driver in London when I met him through some mutual friends. I was invited by a lesbian friend at college to go gay clubbing in London, she was one of those people that had connections everywhere, she knew I was gay - it wasn't a secret at college, however I didn't broadcast it. If someone asked, I would tell them was my approach. I had never done anything like this before, I had just turned sixteen when Paul came on the scene. I was introduced to one of the biggest gay clubs of its time, Astoria also known as G-A-Y. What made this more exciting was that they would have up and coming bands and artists, as well as famous well-known faces perform and go clubbing there in the VIP sections.

The likes of Cher, Madonna and Donna Summer had all made appearances when back in the UK. Boy band Blue was on when I went there, not my kind of music really, but I got involved as you do. They weren't well-known back then and were just getting started with their first hit 'All Rise'.

The place went wild, and it became like a mini concert pushing and shoving to get to the front. When they had finished and left the stage the 'camp-ness' was suddenly upped. Y.M.C.A and all the other gay anthems suddenly came on and got played, it was amazing to see, all different age ranges and walks of life were in there. Drag queens, transgender, those unsure and all in between. Guys as young as fifteen and as old as eighty. All like different colours of the rainbow working as one and shining brightly. It was a community - everyone was there for one thing, to have fun. No one wanted to beat each other up etc., they just wanted to dance the night away. It was a far cry away from the little town pubs I had been used to, in which if you weren't a local you got looked at the wrong way. London seemed to be so open and accepting, it felt like the city that never slept! We didn't leave till about 6.00 am! It felt like the place I needed to be, I had a taste and wanted more...

Nothing really happened straight away with me and Paul. We enjoyed each other's company and had a bit of a laugh that was it really. He seemed a lovely person, but I didn't really fancy him, and I don't think he really fancied me. We stayed friends and got chatting on the internet using what was back in the day MSN Messenger.

As time went on, we stayed in touch and would talk about all sorts of different random stuff. Paul, if you didn't know he was gay came across as quite straight looking and acting. He is interested in football, sports of all kinds, and at the time was a smoker and a drinker. We had very little in common, we were completely yin and yang energy, different ends of the spectrum yet for some reason it worked, and there was a chemistry like an invisible magnet that kept pulling us back to each other.

We got chatting and quite a few months later music got brought up, I mentioned I was jealous he was surrounded by all those theatres and could see whatever show he wanted but to my horror he had never seen a musical in his life!!! I was completely surprised and taken aback. We arranged to meet up again and see a show - this guy needed educating fast. This time however it was more of a date I felt sick to my stomach with nerves. I didn't give too much away to Mum about what was happening, and I got a coach ticket and said I would be staying with friends. As long as I text her often, so she knew I was alive, she wasn't happy but didn't feel she could stop me. Looking back, it was a bit dangerous and I do often think I am so lucky that I was with someone safe. I mean I didn't really know Paul from Adam he could have been a murderer, I don't think it was my smartest move ever, but it was something I had to do. The feeling I had in my gut felt right and was becoming stronger and so intense. I thought 'sod it' I wanted to take a chance.

All we could get tickets for at the time was a new up and coming show 'The Full Monty Musical' we ended up having seats very near the front. The show was fantastic we both loved it and it opened a whole world that was on his doorstep that he never known about. We then went for a stroll in Hyde Park, and had our first kiss in some rather large bushes, not the most romantic of places looking back, but to be honest I didn't care where it was. It felt amazing, natural, so different from when I used to kiss Jennifer and the nightmare braces! It became clear as we got to know each other a little first and things were hotting up - I suddenly found that I was very attracted to Paul.

We went for a pizza near our hotel and we sat outside as it was a hot summer evening. The food came but neither of us felt we could eat much, we were both so nervous, and kept pushing slices of pizza around on the plate. We enjoyed each other's company and then went back to the hotel room. London prices were expensive in the centre, so we made do with a single bed! Not the easiest way to have your first night of wild passion although a challenge we survived and made the best of what we had to work with!

The whole weekend was magical, I felt free and alive, I could be myself without having to hide or mask what I was. We kind of both thought this was just a bit of fun, the logistics weren't too great for a long-term relationship! I lived miles away in the sleepy town of Frome, and he was living it up in London. I guess when cupid's arrow strikes if it's meant to be love will always find a way! While sixteen years on we are still together and going strong and have outlasted a lot of straight friends' relationships.

I do feel Paul is my soul mate, we have both learnt and grown so much from each other and I think we will always be learning and growing. No relationship is easy all the time, we have been through our ups and downs as any couple does. We have seen the good, the bad, and the complete bitch in us both at times. But through it all we have worked and not given up on each other. I feel blessed to have him in my life. He is my rock, not only my partner, my best friend, my life partner. I hope we get to be able to grow old together and eventually retire by the sea, until then I welcome the magic and new adventures in store for us.

06-10-18 – We Had A Hand Fastening to Bind Our Love Forever

Hard Hats at the Ready

Paul and I decided we would give the long-term thing a go, college was over I had survived! The feeling of freedom sunk in and for the first time in however many years I could see light at the end of the tunnel. Mum noticed a change in me, she wasn't sure what was happening, but I seemed happier had a spring in my step. "What goes on in London?" she would often ask. I just used to brush it off "Oh nothing, just friends getting together".

Now the problem I faced was, in order to become a theatre photographer, I needed to get some decent A levels under my belt. I achieved the highest marks for GCSE but needed the A levels to complete the set. Yes, you guessed it, I had to stay on possibly another two to four years to achieve what I needed to! I suddenly felt the light quickly dimming. I decided I would have to just work through it as best as I could. The problem I had was free time wasn't 'photography time' anymore, it was time living my alternative life in London. Paul would borrow his work van and come down and pick me up, then we would leave college and go straight to London. It was exciting, we got up to all sorts of adventures, we would go out shopping in central London, see shows, make love in the back of the van at the Services at halfway point. The world was an exciting place. What I loved about London was that even at 3.00 am in the morning everywhere was open. In Frome you were lucky to find a fish and chip shop open past 10.00 pm!

As time went on the demands of the photography course were becoming too much, and I was starting to fall behind with my work for the first time ever. I spoke with Paul and said I didn't feel like I could commit to the workload. To be fair he always encouraged me to finish the course, he never did A levels and always regretted it and he didn't want me to look back with regrets. I felt I was past the point of no return, if I left college, I could free the shackles and get my life back. I decided to speak to my parents about it. Yet again they were not best pleased, particularly my Dad who said, "Don't throw your life away son". He meant well and cared in his own way, but he sometimes had a bad way of wording things and a habit of making me feel worse than I already did.

I decided I couldn't take the bullying that had continued all the way through and I wanted out of the kids' playground. I spoke to the Headmaster about leaving one Friday before half term, as a rule you had to work at least a week, what was the point, I want out - I made it clear I wasn't impressed. The Headmaster also tried to talk me out of this, saying "What will you do, there aren't many jobs out there you know." I was a bit cheeky and told a white lie "Dad is going to take me on as an apprentice carpenter".

I have always admired the way my Dad loves the work that he does, he is 100% dedicated to his craft, and it shows in his workmanship. I have always felt he was a bit of a wizard for making things. He always told us if you <u>must</u> do something every day, you have to enjoy what you do - this motto has always stuck with me. However, that was just it I wasn't enjoying what I had to do, in fact I was surviving rather than living. I had worked the odd day with my Dad before, but it wasn't really my thing, I used the roof timbers as a Cher stage with real scaffolding! I would tart about and get in the way and slow him down rather than help.

However, I needed an excuse and I told him, "You can phone him if you don't believe me". The Headteacher couldn't be bothered with all that, he wanted to get on home to his own family, the last thing he wanted was to deal with this on a Friday afternoon. He agreed and was happy with the excuse I gave, a few papers to sign and that was it no more college I was FREEEEEEE!!!

My Mum and Dad made it clear that I wouldn't be lazing about the house, I was expected to get a job and fast. I wrote letters to different local photographers of all kinds to see if I could get a job or apprenticeship, but no one wanted me.

I ended up getting a job in Dairy Crest cheese factory, it wasn't the best job in the world, very mundane picking and packing on the line with the girls. However, I was young and the pay cheque at the end of the week made up for the boredom. Soon I was earning a nice little income which made weekends away in London even better! Not only did we get to see shows we could squeeze in two a day and go clubbing until the early hours!

It must have been about six or seven months into my time at Dairy Crest and me and Paul got chatting. "Why don't you move in with me and my flat mates?" Paul lived at the top of a block of flats with two other lads. It wasn't the most glamorous of places, but it did the job, it was next to Northolt train station and the track was right opposite the flat. Every time a train went past, the whole block of flats would shake and wobble and you were always a little unsure if it was going to survive. The odd time I questioned if it would go down like a pack of dominoes.

The problem I had with moving away was that my Dad still didn't have a clue as to what was going on. He knew at this time that I had a male friend but that was all. This was an awkward time to say the least, I spoke to Mum about it and she agreed it might be for the best. She would miss me like crazy but Dad and myself had been locking horns a lot lately, there was a lot of tension in the air and a storm was brewing. Perhaps some time away might be what is needed, despite me bringing in my own money, he seemed very down on me. It felt like whatever I was doing was just not good enough and I think he couldn't get passed me walking away from college, a decision that wasn't made lightly. Dad really enjoyed his own school days and would often say he wished he could relive them. For me, and my mum who had it hard with her own school days, it was a living hell. Because he had never been through it, he didn't know how to respond to it.

We told Dad that I was going to go to London to pursue my options as a theatre photographer. This wasn't a lie this was still the end goal, although I think I knew at the time this was now unreachable. However still optimistic I thought I had nothing to lose. He agreed I could go on one condition... he wanted to personally meet Paul...

Visiting a Cave in Cornwall

Playing it Straight

I felt a mix of emotions, I was excited to have the nod I could move to London, but in sheer panic at Dad having to meet Paul. It wasn't that we wanted to hide what we were about, it was that we all knew how Dad would respond. He just couldn't get his head around the fact you can't help who you fall in love with. Some people are born gay, it's no one else's business what anyone is. As long as your child is fit and healthy, then that is a true blessing and everything else is secondary. However, we all knew Dad wasn't going to see it that way.

I debriefed Paul before he went inside to meet my parents, the brief was we were merely friends and that was all. I was going to London to jump start my photography career. My dad started his Spanish inquisition the moment Paul's feet hit the doormat and for the first time ever football came in handy. Paul loved all sports and the topic of football quickly became mutual ground. My Dad and Paul bonded over sports and my Dad could see all would be OK and I would be with someone safe and OK. Happy with all the questions ticked on his list, I gave my notice with Dairy Crest and packed my worldly goods ready for a new life in London.

This was a huge deal for me at the time, whilst others were still studying at college, I was off exploring the bright lights in the 'big smoke'. I said my goodbyes to Mum, Dad and my sister, "I will miss you all like crazy", we all had tears rolling down our cheeks. It was the hardest thing moving away, but it was needed for all involved at the time, myself and Paul became a proper couple and got to know everything about each other. Life was magical, and full of dreams and adventures to be had.

A few days later Mum phoned me in a bit of a panic, she was great at keeping secrets if she had to, I swear she could have been a spy. But she also was only human and there was only so much she could take. She got into a bit of an argument with my Dad over something silly, and like a volcano ready to erupt out came the words "your son is gay!" I wasn't there and probably for the best, from what Mum and Hazel told me, Dad's face turned a shade of white and grey and he couldn't speak for a whole week. The shit had well and truly hit the fan.

Mum apologised but also said it was stupid walking around on eggshells, it was indeed stupid! I should be able to live my life the way I saw fit, I wasn't breaking any laws, I was still the same and nothing had changed. Mum said to Dad "looking back, surely you could see the signs?" Everyone could see the signs if they looked hard enough, some just wanted to bury their heads in the sand. I think me being in London was the best thing to happen, Dad had time away and could think and reflect on everything.

Suddenly, all the mood swings and locking of horns with each other made sense, Dad wasn't impressed about my life style choices, however he didn't want to lose his son and he was in a 'catch 22'! I had already moved out so if he choose to shut the door on me that would be it, gone! We spoke on the phone and he wanted me to be sure I *was* gay, I was! He then assured me it would be hard for him but he would support me the best way he could. He wasn't happy about it but knew he had no other option.

Dad has always been there for me and now looks at Paul more like a second son. He will never be 100% comfortable with it, but that unconditional love between a father and son was stronger to him than anything else. He drives me insane at times, and he probably thinks the same of me, but I think the world of him and love him unconditionally. I want to thank him for allowing me to be the person I am. You may not understand me and that's ok, but you will always stand with me and never try to block my pathway, and for this there aren't enough words and 'thank you' just doesn't seem enough.

Me Dressed Up For Rocky Horror Show

Bright Lights and Big City

London for me was a magical place back then, I really saw it as the city that didn't sleep. You could smell it before you touched base, the big smoke - and it was with the strong smell of pollution filling the air and grand tall buildings full of history and secrets. I was seventeen and thought I was living the high life whilst others were still at college in a classroom! I managed to save a small amount of money from Dairy Crest to form some savings - this wouldn't last long. Champagne taste on a cider pocket springs to mind, I was young, naive and a little bit stupid.

I felt I needed to experience London, it definitively was the place I was able to grow, it shaped me and opened my eyes to the real world around me, but also sexually and within myself. I had no restrictions, I was able to find myself again and quickly felt that inner peace inside me. Me and Paul could come and go from the flat as we pleased and the world, within reason, really was our oyster.

The plan was to get some work and pick up from where I left off. The theatre photography was still hanging by a thread in the background, but for now any job would do. Work seemed a bit harder to come by for me up there. I couldn't drive so had to rely on public transport and I spent the first month or so trying to understand the buses and tube layouts.

I spent time just applying for job after job and I was lucky if I would hear back from any, the ones I did hear from were to say 'thanks but no thanks'. This started to bring me down quickly and London was becoming a little bit harder to survive in. Paul was worried I was starting to become a bit depressed and fed up and he suggested short term, why don't I ride with him in the van? It seemed a good idea to me, I would end up seeing the sights and possibly get a job en route.

The plan was Paul had to load the van before he could leave site and do whatever route was on for the day, this literally would change daily. Some days we would be in central London and be finished by 1.00 pm so could go off and see a show afterwards and have a spot of lunch somewhere. Other times we might have to go as far out as Guildford or Kent, so we wouldn't get home till about 5.00 pm or 6.00 pm.

I would meet him at a little bridge around the corner from his work, he had to be very careful as he was putting his job at risk by me being with him. Driving has always made me feel very sleepy, whether I'm driving myself or being a passenger. I was finding on the longer drives I would start to fall asleep, this became a bit of a deadly pattern, and by about 2.00 pm if we were on a long run, I would be asleep for the most part.

Looking back Paul should have really sat me down and said, "enough now". Without meaning to I was becoming selfish and taking the piss and taking advantage of the situation and Paul's good nature. The problem was we enjoyed each other's company and we wanted it to work and didn't want to give up on each other. We decided to split the week, with the first part spent job searching and Thursday and Friday being 'van' days. I continued with my job search but was getting nowhere fast.

Over time the novelty of London was starting to lose its shine, I have always seen London a little bit like a pyramid with three sides. Those that are stinking rich, those that are on the breadline, and those that fall somewhere in the middle - I felt as if I was tapping into all three but was a master of none. I would still chat to my Mum a lot on the phone as I didn't really have many friends that were about in the day, surprise they all had jobs! Mum would offer words of encouragement, but it was becoming clear that I was quite homesick. I had never been away from home before, and things were starting to take their toll on me.

I stayed in London for around five to six months in total and it just felt like I couldn't crack the puzzle. I had seen past London's outside beauty and the rose-tinted glasses had fallen. Back in Somerset there was a lot of green countryside and you don't have to go far to walk and think. I was feeling denied of mother earth's embrace, and a witch cannot survive without nature! London was different, you had to be careful where you went wandering off to, whilst there were some lovely places about with green land, you couldn't always get to them without a car.

I was starting to miss the simpler life that Somerset offered. Tall buildings, congested roads, loud noise and people everywhere were starting to take their toll on me. I felt as if my energy levels had become invaded by everything around me, and I was being pulled down by negative muggle energy everywhere. What I once saw as my escape and a shiny palace, was fast becoming a cage around me and I felt like its prisoner.

Dad to the Rescue

On occasion, I would go back and visit my family in Frome, this involved a few things, lots of hugs and kisses, but also a good talking to and fattening up with Mum's proper home cooking.

London was a strange place and I guess mine and Paul's relationship was a bit weird. Whilst we were out and proud on my side Paul was still in the closet and none of his family knew about us! London was a big place and it was known for putting on a show. You could show people what you wanted them to see and hide what you didn't a lot more easily up there. I would often get very annoyed about this but knew it was something only Paul could tackle as and when he felt ready. Rushing him or putting pressure would end up killing the relationship which I didn't want to happen.

He would sometimes nip round to see his parents and I would be left in the flat alone, he'd be gone for some time making me go wild with anger. It was clear he had food whilst there and he tried to make it up to me by buying me junk food. I had never experienced an Indian curry until I met Paul or scrambled egg for that matter, they were things my family didn't like so we never tried them. It would take more than a curry to resolve this, I started to feel like history was repeating itself, I didn't want to be someone's dirty little secret and I felt I was being pulled backwards in time rather than moving forward.

Whilst on a visit back home, Dad could see I didn't seem myself, so I explained some of my frustrations. He suggested, "would it be better if you moved back home?", whilst I was struggling, I didn't want to break up with Paul, but he didn't mean that. "Why don't you both move down here and make a go of it?" he asked. "You can stay here short term until you find somewhere to live". Was I hearing this right? Dad seemed to have gone full circle. Mum let slip he was worrying a lot more about me then he let on and missed me being around. I suggested the idea to Paul but was pretty sure it would be a flat 'no', he had his friends and family, a good job with decent income and would be giving up a lot more than I did to move away. To my surprise and without any persuasion, he was completely up for the idea. I think London life had also taken its toll and he was ready for some new adventures himself.

Once more we packed up and Paul said his goodbyes. He promised to see his family regularly when he could, and that was it - off we went back to sunny Somerset. As we were driving down the air felt a little cleaner, the grass glowed a little greener, for me I felt like I was coming back home and where I should be, mother earth was welcoming us back with open arms.

I still smile on my adventures in London - it was indeed a magical place. I learnt so much about life whilst there. But for me the hustle and bustle were too much, I am happy to visit for the odd day or weekend, but I'm always glad when it's time to leave and come back out again.

Father and Son Love

Driving

We settled into life in Frome pretty quickly, Paul took a while to adjust to a quiet pace of life, but in his own way I think he enjoyed it. He did miss friends and family, but he was older and had been living on his own for some time so was able to cope. There was one rule of thumb with living under Dad and Mum's roof, no funny business! This was hard for both me and Paul, in London we weren't governed by any rules, we could do what we want as and when we wanted. We had to start to get a bit creative with where we would play, woods and other discrete locations became play areas for us through our times of sexual frustration.

We both got jobs, neither of us felt they were great, but it was money coming in and we could use this to build up the pot. I ended up working for a little photo and dry-cleaning booth inside Sainsburys. I was bored, the average day involved reading a book a lot of the time, but it was a job. Mum would end up running me to and from work, and on occasion Paul. This wasn't ideal, Dad decided the time was coming when I needed to learn to drive, he agreed to pay for lessons. I was very wary of driving; the whole idea scared the hell out of me. I just didn't feel I would be very good, it seemed very technical. I refused for quite some time until one day Mum wasn't able to pick me up and I had no choice but to walk. To make matters worse it was hammering down with rain and I had no coat, that was it, where are my L plates?

I agreed with Dad that I would learn to drive on one condition, I decided who my driving instructor would be. He reluctantly agreed, and I started researching female driving instructors within the area. I knew I was going to be a nervous driver and I always found at school the female teachers were easier to open up with and I felt instantly more relaxed. I think this is possibly to do with their energy just being more balanced. I had a past life regression years later and was a female witch in one lifetime, so this might explain why I felt more comfortable with feminine energy. I also had an astrology reading and it came to light I have a large area that has crone energy within it. My experience with some male teachers had not been great, and the last thing I needed was a homophobic driving instructor.

We eventually found a lovely more mature lady in Westbury, Wiltshire called Sandra. I booked her, and she turned up a few days later in her gold Renault Clio, we got chatting and off we went. I was very slow on the first run out and felt like I was all over the place. I found her easy to talk to and as time went on, we formed a nice little friendship. We would often chat about things none driving related, she was firm but fair but also put me at ease quickly.

Sandra suggested I book in to do my theory test, I did so and passed first time. That was half the battle over I thought. People are interesting, I know some that are great drivers but took ages to nail the theory side, and vice versa. For me this was easy and straight forward it was the driving part I wasn't so keen on.

Whilst I was doing OK with the lessons, Sandra did suggest that to speed the process up it might be handy to have a car of my own to practice in. I was only having one lesson per week so there was a long gap between sessions. Dad looked at putting me on his car insurance, but prices were not cheap. I also wasn't overly keen on this idea, Dad's Honda Accord he had at the time was double the size of what I was used to driving in.

My Nan and Grampy (Dad's parents) had moved in next door. They had been living in Oldfield Park in Bath for most of their life but decided the parking was becoming a nightmare and their family home was too big. The house next door to Mum and Dad had gone up for sale, it was smaller than where my Nan and Grampy currently lived, but big enough for what they needed. They moved in and enjoyed a more relaxed approach to life then the hustle and bustle of Bath.

My Dad and Grampy got talking about this car business. They decided to go halves and get me my own first car, this was exciting I had to say! I really enjoyed the little Renault Clio so something like that would be perfect! The only problem was both Dad and Grampy did not like French cars, they were Ford and Honda gentleman. It was made clear I wouldn't be having anything too flash or French as chances were, I might have a bump in the first couple of years. All three of us went off around the garages but nothing was ticking the boxes, either too expensive, too big, overpriced, or too foreign. Both Dad and Grampy were like peas in a pod, cut from the same cloth and when they got together it was definitely double trouble!

We were in the last garage this was basically the make or break to getting a car on that particular day. They both loved to haggle and would rather walk away from a deal if they couldn't get it on their terms, so they could keep their pride. I didn't and still don't understand that mindset, if you want something sometimes you have to pay the price. It was very 50/50 if we would even get anything until there she was in the corner, a lovely Renault Clio. She was in budget and a lovely shade of purple, what more could I ask for? My Dad started asking the dealer questions, he didn't look impressed. Does it have a CD player was all I was worried about and power steering, Dad decided with the backup of Grampy that it was a no go!

That was that then I thought but they both started getting rather excited about a car next to the Clio. An older looking white Rover Metro - it had a tape player and manual steering! The boys weren't selling it to me. We took it for a spin, it had a strange smell which I thought was damp possibly connected with the sunroof? "No, no", the car dealer started to spin his web of lies "no damp in here, just needs a good run and bit of airing where it has sat still." Hmmm I wasn't sure this was the one for me. I wasn't being ungrateful, but it was important I felt a little bit happy with the purchase, as it would be me driving the thing. It was ending up that or nothing, so I took my chances and agreed - I was now the proud owner of a N reg Rover Metro Kensington limited addition!

The First Car I Ever Owned

Seventh Time Lucky

Gut feelings never lie! I started to learn how to drive the Metro or "beast" as I called it. The lovely purchase in summer was perfect, however winter was a different story and as I had first thought it did indeed leak! This made learning to drive a little harder as depending on what corner you turned, you may get water droplets on you if it had been raining. This wasn't ideal, but Dad wanted me to ignore all that and focus on the task in hand. I wish, looking back, someone had shown me how to protect myself spiritually. A bubble of protection or mirrored shields would have done the trick, I think I might have cracked this driving lark a little sooner!

I loved my Dad and was grateful for the purchase, the problem I had was he was a little less patient than Sandra, and we also didn't have the luxury of dual control! The brakes in Sandra's car were sharp, you only had to tap them, and you would nearly be sent through the window! The brakes on this car took longer to kick in so it was important to allow extra stopping time. Needless to say, we had a few close calls! That wasn't the only issue I was having... the steering was manual and whilst overall wasn't too bad, parking of any kind was very, very heavy! We would often go out for an evening drive, sometimes we did OK, but nine times out of ten Dad would do my head in, and he would probably say the same about me. He was trying to show me short cuts and questioned the way I was driving, I was driving the way the professional and the one that ultimately will get me through my test had shown me.

It seemed like he was trying to know better than the teacher and would often say "I would do it this way", Sandra very early on spotted a problem with having two cars. It was basically like I had two teachers with yin and yang energy showing itself once more. Sandra would sometimes use visualizations to help me focus. An example was when I was very heavy with the pedals, she suggested - imagine the clutch and accelerator are like a seashore ride, as one goes up the other gently goes down. This made sense to me, she showed me in a way I could relate to. Dad on the other hand was trying his best but we were just clashing way too much, he would often raise his voice getting louder and louder thinking he could shout his methods at me to learn his way.

I tended to get a lot of headaches whilst learning to drive. For some reason it seemed to activate my third eye and on top of that I felt like spirit were once again nudging me to work with them! This was very inappropriate I had to say in my thoughts… 'enough, stop and leave me alone!' The problem was they had already left me alone for a little while and once again where trying their luck.

Whilst I was learning to drive, I got a new job at Coopers in Westbury, a family run supermarket. The job was working on the deli counter and it was more pay, a lot of people told me they didn't want to do the work, but it was good money and a full-time wage. I now needed to 'nail' this driving business more than ever, I didn't want to have to rely on lifts and public transport for too long.

Sandra decided we book my first test in - it was a wash out I knew I had failed straight away by doing a major wrong error. Two more times we booked and again both times failed! The problem I was having was whilst I could drive perfectly well when it came to the test the nerves were getting the better of me and I didn't seem to be able to control them!

We left it for a bit, but Sandra had some other welcome news, she knew me and Paul were looking for a place to live. I explained I was working at Coopers and wasn't keen on the travelling. It wasn't so much the travel itself, it was more a case of public transport around the area was poor - not like in London where there was a bus every five minutes. Sandra explained she was renting out a flat she had, and might we be interested, I felt immediately like this was already ours the gut feeling was once again so strong! I hadn't even seen it yet, so we arranged a viewing and it ticked all the boxes, it was done to a high level spec and it had the 'wow' factor. We moved in a couple of weeks later. Getting to and from work was resolved, I was able to walk! It was only a ten-minute walk up the road, me and Paul felt like we could breathe again and had our freedom back.

It took me several more attempts to try and crack this driving but once again the nerves kicked in. I decided on the seventh go this was make or break and would be my last attempt, I was starting to really dislike driving before I had even begun! For some reason I asked and sent a prayer out to my Grampy to watch over me and help me with this. If he could, I hoped he could hear my plea, the test started and once again I thought I had messed up. I think what this did was allow me to relax I waited to hear that I had failed again and have Sandra drive me home which was what happened when you didn't pass 'the drive home of shame' - but no OMG I had only gone and done it!

I believed my Grampy had indeed played his part, and like he had always done before, when I asked for help it was given. I thanked him, and thought to myself why didn't I ask him sooner? More proof that the spirit world had not left my side and were still there waiting for me in the background.

I looked up the significance of seven as it had taken me seven attempts. This seemed to make sense to me:

"The number 7 is the seeker, the thinker, the searcher of TRUTH. The 7 doesn't take anything at face value - it is always trying to understand the underlying, hidden truths. The 7 knows that nothing is exactly as it seems, and that reality is often hidden behind illusions."

Relief – Legally Allowed at the Wheel

A Little Shop Called Coopers

Coopers was a strange place to work. It was an old-fashioned family run supermarket. More than half of Westbury seemed to work there or had worked there at some point.

The deli counter tended to be my domain, it was an interesting job. I can't say I always enjoyed it, but you certainly got to meet a mixed bag of the general public. When it was busy there would be more than one of us working on the counter. The problem was people can be very rude and impatient some of the older customers wanted to have a bit of a chinwag and chat, whilst you weighed out their ox tongue for them. For a lot of them it was their only form of socialising, I tried to give good banter but multi task and keep the queue flowing. You would always get one idiot that would want to whinge because you were making small talk and slowing down their day!

You literally had to have hands everywhere, cutting on the meat slicers, cutting cheese, sanitising your hands in between. Working on the deli counter my hands did become quite rough, it was a lot more physical than people realise. Gathering meats and cheeses of a morning in the freezing cold walk-in fridge and then cutting it throughout the day. Dismantling the slicing machine to clean it at the end of the day plus the dreaded chicken roaster, it literally would collect chicken fat and God knows what else.

I got on and got my hands dirty but over time they were starting to become very sore and rough and would easily cut open. Not helped by certain cheeses that you would have to cut, the dreaded Parmesan cheese being the worst offender. You literally had to have arms of steel to cut through a huge slab of the stuff, I would close my eyes whilst running the cheese wire down through. It was guaranteed eight times out of ten to snap and almost take your eye out! Customers would 'tut' away as you then had to change the wire and try again. I decided that this was just more trouble than it's worth so would often say, if it was asked for it was out of stock. It wasn't worth losing my eyes for as when the wire snapped it would literally spring up and would often break in your face. My eyesight was worth more than a bit of cheese that smelt like sick I thought.

I later got moved to the bakery section, the opportunity rose to learn how to be the local baker in there and I was taken on as Assistant Manager. Not much to it really as more than half the stuff was frozen, or part baked, more a case of warming things up. You had to attend to the fresh bread and the pre-sliced stuff that would come in from Hovis and other brands, so you would be out the front and out the back in equal measures.

Yet again spirit where making themselves known to me - the bakery section was haunted. My shift was an early start and I would be in at 6.00 am putting the bread delivery out and lots of weird things would happen. Next to the bakery entrance was a lift, that went directly up to the butchery section above. I would come out of the bakery and there would be a cage blocking the pathway with full pig carcasses on them, blood would leak out everywhere and the only way you would get past was to either move the cage out if there was space in the warehouse, or jump over it and pray you didn't fall flat on top, face to face with a dead pig staring back at you!

The bakery was a pretty active place, I would be wrapping the fresh bread, and could see out onto the shop floor. The pre-sliced stuff had all been put out and looked ready for when the doors would open at 7.00 am. Loaves of bread would throw themselves off the shelf randomly for no reason! We also had baskets for fresh rolls, cheese baps, doughnuts and more... often I would fill this up nip for a tea break and come back again all before the store was open. The baskets would all be switched around facing different ways! This was most odd, there was only a handful of us in the building at the time, and I knew where they all were so they could not have done anything. It didn't scare me I just used to get a bit frustrated! The job involved a lot of multi-tasking between about ten different ovens, a freezer and prover, so I didn't need the added fun and games the spirit world seemed to like to throw at me.

Other weird happenings would occur on a regular basis, the lift outside the bakery that took you up to the butchers, which was only suitable for carrying stock and it wasn't safe enough for people to travel up in. You would often hear this go up and down of its own accord, you would then hear the butchers coming in, with their meat delivery wondering why the lift was upstairs and looking rather puzzled when no one had been up there yet. I would often hear like I had done in art and photography classes at college, whisperings - I couldn't always make it out but there was a lot of gossiping going on from the spirit world it seemed. There was also a lot of gossiping going on, on the shop floor...

I was the training Assistant Manager of the bakery department. I worked alongside my Manager, an Essex lady for purposes of the book we will call Lady Crumble. Lady Crumble was an interesting character to say the least, loud and lewd at times, we became quite close and she confided in me with personal matters. I really cared and had a lot of time for Lady Crumble, the problem was it felt at times like she was two people and you didn't always know which one you would see on your shift.

Sometimes she would come into work and be really bouncy and a pleasure to be around. Other days she would come in and she might not talk to you till 2.00 pm in the afternoon, leaving you wondering what you had said or done. That was just it, you hadn't done or said anything, from conversations we had it was clear she had a dark past. A hard time with her Mum and an abusive previous marriage. However, she failed to see that was her past and she had survived, to make matters worse she was also going through the menopause.

As time went on, I was struggling with the constant negative energy I was finding myself in, it was like Lady Crumble was becoming a psychic vampire, (although I was unaware of the concept back then). I decided the time for a new job was now, but she begged me not to go and, the owners also didn't want me to leave yet. A meeting and pay rise were put in place and so I stayed on. However, this as I learned would come at a cost.

When people start to value you and your self-worth, the ugly green-eyed monster can rear its head and get in the way. People for whatever reason suddenly felt threatened and jealous by the fact I had been asked to stay and a pay rise was issued. We tried to keep things as discrete as possible, but as anyone who has worked in any form of retail knows, people like to gossip.

I carried on regardless - I wasn't going to apologise for being good at my job, if people had an issue tough, 'that was their monkey to deal with and not mine' I thought. The directors of the company were very hands on and had decided they wanted to take a back seat, a new manager was put in place and the first three months of him being there his role was to study and learn all aspects of the team, and their involvement.

I like to give everyone a fair chance, treat me with respect and you will get the same back. Upon meeting this new store manager, without him even saying a word a feeling of dread and discomfort came over me. In later years with my mediumship I learnt a lot about energy, auras and magnetic fields around people. For whatever reason which I would soon discover, the energy field around us was clashing big time. I took an instant dislike to him, I felt a little harsh, as he hadn't done anything, but I felt sick to my stomach! Whilst I had no idea why, I was becoming very in tune with things, and so took this as some kind of warning.

All the other managers seemed to be swarming around him like a pack of flies around a big turd. For a lot of them all self-respect had gone out the window. They saw him as someone who had power, he could help them up the ladder, something they had wanted! When they became envious of me getting rewarded for my own actions, they wanted that acknowledgement without putting the hard graft work in.

As time went on it was clear he was VERY homophobic. My gut feeling had indeed been a warning to me. He decided that managers and assistant managers needed to be reviewed monthly. My review went well my work was solid so there was nothing he could pull me up on, this seemed to bug him. He started calling in on managers only, it was clear they were to become his spies on the shop floor. Again, it stunk of depression, and these idiots would rather chuck you under a bus if it meant they got a step up the ladder and possible pay rise!

Some little snake in the grass let slip that I had used to work on the deli counter and wasn't always so keen on it. He decided to put me back on there on a temporary basis as my contract stated I was to work in the bakery, the only two people that knew how to run the bakery where myself and Lady Crumble. This meant the bakery would take a hit, Lady Crumble's son who only worked on weekends also knew how to run the bakery section.

It was as if I had gone backwards in time. Whilst on the deli they had changed the way they had done stuff to when I had been working there. I soon picked up where I had left off. It was clear they were trying to force me out. I also had seen cracks with how this new system seemed to work. Things were taking double the time, and there seemed to be no structure so I decided to explain my findings to him. Surely, he was a businessman, and it made sense that he should be getting the most from all departments of the business he was overseeing.

Sadly, I was shouted down before I could even explain my point, where had this outburst of aggression come from, I thought to myself, I had done nothing to him. The problem I had and have found since on my journey, is sometimes when you know who you are mind, body and spirit, people feel threatened by that. They don't know how to deal with it, as they can't control you and so you hold the power over them. He knew to me that he was just another cog in the wheel, I wasn't going to roll over on his every whim and request and he didn't know how to handle that.

I carried on regardless. Part of my new role back on the deli included doing late nights till 8.00 pm! This was a complete waste of time, you saw a handful of people if you were lucky. The only bonus with this was that my shift would start at 11.00 am so I had a lie in. Often Paul would come in and we would chat for a while and kill some time.

I did however used to see a lovely older lady, she would come in every Friday and buy scraps of meat or 'off cuts' as they were known for her dogs. Being that it was late there was no long queue of people, so I had time to chat to her freely and she helped make the evening go a little quicker. One Friday night she came in and could see I was low, she didn't pry or ask any questions, she merely looked at me with a smile and reminded me of the motto my Dad had. "If you have to do something every day you have to enjoy what you do". She then added "your face is making it clear a new adventure is required". With that she bid me farewell until next Friday.

Next Friday came but sadly, she never turned up, the same thing happened the following week. I then learned through the gossipmongers that she had sadly passed away peaceful in her sleep, I was saddened to hear this and a little shocked to be honest. I replayed the words she had said to me, had she been sent from the higher realms? I decided she was right I was wasting my time in a world that no longer wanted me. I spoke to Paul about it, and whilst he was VERY wary he didn't want me to suffer in silence.

I handed my notice in, I only had to give a week by law although they preferred a month, 'tough' I thought, a week was what they were getting. People sometimes ask me why I didn't fight a little harder, go to the HR department. The problem was with it being a small family run business, you couldn't really go to anyone as they all worked together, and managers had each other's backs. I also had no fight left to give, I had been all through that with school days and wasn't going to start again now.

My final week arrived, I thought it would be simple enough, but they made it ten times more difficult than it needed to be. No one in the canteen would speak when I was on lunch break and I once again found myself outside a circle looking in... On the last day Lady Crumble shot me a look, shoved a good luck card in my hand and that was it. She walked off alongside the Store Manager as if she had just taken out the trash?

Four and a half years of hard graft and for what I thought, it was a bittersweet affair. In many ways it was a job that I really enjoyed and looking back now prior to the latter months one of the best I have had. Still, the feeling of freedom and relief came over me. The world once more was my oyster...

My First Real Experience of the Retail World

Divine Timing

You are probably starting to see in my journey that divine timing has always played its part. The days of Coopers were done, I had no idea what I was going to do next, but just the feeling of freedom and inner peace was a welcome relief.

I knew that I was done with retail for a while and ideally wanted to turn my attention towards something creative, it didn't take long to find a new job. This came very out of the blue; my Dad's friend had a brother who owned his own model making business. They specialised in making architectural models for building developments, as well as some high-end life-size models for various things including racing car models for the likes of McLaren. (Due to a contract I signed, and them having some very high-end clientele I am not able to legally name them all in this book.)

This company however ticked all the boxes. The chance to be creative, Monday to Friday 8.00 am until 4.00 pm with optional overtime and weekends free! This really seemed like I had struck gold and landed on my feet. They knew from conversations that my Dad had already had with them that I was "arty", and they wanted someone who could paint some of the small cars and intricate pieces that went on these new development models.

The plan was they would take me on as an apprentice and I ended up with a similar pay to what I was earning at Coopers. This was probably the job I enjoyed the most, a bit awkward at first, the team was made up of men of all different ages and one woman. Yet again the 'age old' conversation around sexuality briefly raised its head, some were a bit old school around it, but no one was offensive. I was being hired and employed for my talents and nothing else was important - this felt like a breath of fresh air. Guys that respected me for me and just let me get on and be. What I also loved about working there was no uniform, you could wear what you wanted, you just had to knuckle down to the task in hand. You could even listen to music on headphones the whole day as long as the work got done.

About three months in I was busy at my workstation painting away when I suddenly received a phone call on my mobile, yes, we could even take calls at work! The lady on the phone introduced herself as Manager of the fruit and vegetable section of Coopers - strange as her voice sounded very familiar. She asked if I was interested in becoming the Bakery Manager? hmmm let me think, I wasn't being rude or difficult, but I am a firm believer once you have left somewhere you never go back so I made it clear I was not interested.

The sound of panic in her voice as she continued to try and sell it to me, from what she didn't say it was clear it was Lady Crumble and she wanted me to go back! Not because she wanted me there, she obviously wanted to expand the fruit and vegetable department but there was a catch - she now was the only person who knew how to run the bakery. She was never going to be able to progress to a different department until others learnt her role, something she would find difficult as it would mean giving up some of her "power". I found this extremely disrespectful under the circumstances and I asked that she never call me again, that was it, she was out of my life. But this time on my terms - I had taken out the rubbish. Coopers had really affected my confidence and where London had allowed me to bloom, Coopers towards the end set me back within myself. So again, I was becoming quiet and shy.

I vowed when I left Coopers I would never venture back inside, and I didn't even to get shopping, Paul would go in alone and get the weekly shop. He has always found it easier to stand his ground and he wasn't going to be insulted or pushed around by anybody.

The weeks went quickly in the new job, I found I was loving it and loving life. Paul and I were able to do stuff at weekends, suddenly the constrictions had gone, and life was enjoyable. It really was a pleasant time for me, I slowly started chatting to the guys there, and they would help me start to rebuild my confidence.

I should be happy, I was happy, but at the same time something didn't feel quite right. I couldn't put my finger on it, but it almost felt like I was waiting for the other shoe to drop...

Feather of Protection

Castle.... With a View

About four months prior to leaving Coopers my ex driving instructor and now landlady Sandra had some news - she needed to let the flat go. Maintenance costs for the outside areas of the flat building were becoming increasingly high and she didn't feel she was getting a great return.

She wanted to show us a new property she had purchased, if we liked it, we could move in, and it would be ours to rent and look after. We went along to 13 Castle View in Westbury for a look, but first impressions were not particularly great. Whilst it was OK, it felt a little small and in need of a bit of TCL, the flat had some lovely big rooms and it was light and airy. It did have a lovely big conservatory and long narrow garden, we had never had a garden before, so this was a welcome addition. The bedrooms and kitchen seemed a lot smaller, however.

"I'll leave you boys to discuss and have a think?" she said. We felt so torn... we loved the little flat, but she made it clear that was going. We started looking around at other options, but nothing was jumping out at us. So, despite this house feeling smaller and costing slightly more money, we agreed it made sense long term. We know where we stood with Sandra and she with us, she knew we were good tenants that would look after the place and keep it nice and in check.

It couldn't have been that bad as we ended up moving in and staying there for twelve years! The home had indeed grown on us like mould. What I did love about it, was it was directly below the famous Westbury White Horse and as you drive towards it you could see the hill behind you in the background. I always felt like the white chalked horse had magical power and was watching over us a bit like a guardian protector from the animal world. In the summer it was particularly nice driving past, as you would often see people on the top of the hill hand gliding, all different colour hand gliders would be in the sky and they formed their own rainbow.

Funny how you don't always appreciate what you have until it's gone, me and Paul on occasion would whinge and moan about that little house as it certainly wasn't without its problems - different types of leaking being one. Cowboy builders were called in to patch up the damage. The bath had a shower inside, but due to it forming a leak Sandra decided to rip this out, this was a harsh blow for both of us. We loved a shower, but we equally loved a good soak in the bath, I think I was a merman in a previous lifetime or realm.

A new slimline walk-in shower was installed, this was great for a time, but again the leaking started once more, and this time was coming into the kitchen. We continued to have problems on and off until the day we had to leave. Looking back now it does make me chuckle at some of things we had to go through, but at the time it wasn't funny! The electricity was on a key meter and quite often I would be singing away in the shower when the key would run out of money and I would be plunged into darkness. I had to sneak down in just a towel to put the emergency meter on. Looking back now it does make me laugh, but at the time it used to make me so cross and you would hear all the names under the sun!

We were lucky enough to share some amazing adventures whilst in that home, so I do feel entirely blessed to say I lived at the Castle with a View.

My Garden in the Peak of Summer 2015

The Other Shoe....

For the first time in a long time it felt like life was flowing as it was meant to. The new home at Castle View had finally had a bit of a facelift before we moved in. Me and Paul continued to blossom and loved the adventures we were having as a couple. Life seemed simple, easy, the job was going well, and I was loving the fact I could tap into my creative energy. It even felt like the spirit world had calmed down around me and left me alone to just enjoy being. I guess all good things must come to an end!

Then one Monday morning at work I found myself in an emergency meeting. We were heading into the winter months around November time and it was starting to get quite a bit colder and mornings would bring thick ice on the car window, and signs that Jack Frost had made his presence known. There was a feeling of bitterness and unease in the air.

The meeting was with the two Directors of the business, they announced it was with regret that they had to let me, and two others go! The company was struggling a little more than anyone was aware of and to keep afloat some redundancies had to be made. To say I was gutted was an understatement, it wasn't only a job I enjoyed doing, I felt for the first time I was making something of my life. My Dad even seemed to show some emotion and some feelings of open proudness for this first time in what felt like forever.

It felt like the rug was being pulled out from underneath me. They said they would pay me until January and I could leave to look for work, they really were sorry and had there been another way around it they would have kept me on. I could see they were just as upset delivering the news. I still felt I was blessed to have learnt and experienced what they did show me.

Once again it was time to look for something new, the problem now was I had lots of commitments. I couldn't afford to be fussy but... I still had a bitter feeling from Coopers, it was suggested I go back with my tail between my legs. Out of the question, for me that bridge was well and truly burnt! I had a feeling all would be OK - you think by now I would have started to listen to all these feelings!

Well everything did turn out OK, I ended up back in retail, but this time a little higher end. I was taken on by a German company that had a chain of furniture retail departments to work in the beds part of the business which was a completely separate company, but the franchise owned both.

I ended up learning everything and I mean everything there is to know about beds and mattresses, pillows and all the extras that went with it. Days would be filled with redressing beds in the showroom and ironing bed linen, speaking to customers and trying to get them to purchase products. The job was commission based with a flat rate wage with it this meant that depending how many sales you made you could earn a fair number of pennies in a month.

The job was straightforward, my style of selling was and has always been to be yourself. There's nothing worse than walking into a store and having the salesperson pounce on you before you have even stepped inside, I personally hated that approach so why would the customers feel any different. I decided the best way was to greet them of a morning and them leave them to it, if they had any questions they knew where to find me.

This tactic on the whole should of and did at times work really well - there was just one problem! I was entering, although I didn't realise it, a very cold materialistic world that was full of jealously, egotistic, money driven, self-greed energies. Of course, I wasn't aware of this at the time, had I known I would have walked away before I started. Cue my work colleague... For the purposes of the book we will call her... Madame Short Temper.

Psychic Vampire Number Two

The team was only small, made up of three of us and it felt like we had the good, the normal, and the downright ugly. The Manager was a mature gentleman who had been in sales all his life and wanted something a little slower which this was. He had a heart of gold and was really too nice for the job, then there was me that was wanting to learn and just get on with the work in hand. There were no dramas when me and the Manager worked together, we both knew what needed doing, and worked as a team to achieve this.

The problem however was to my left, Madam Short Temper... she was and still is one of the most bizarre creatures I have ever worked alongside. Never one to reveal how old she actually was I would guess late fifties no older than sixty, but she would have you believe she was a lot younger!

She looked like an old Betty Boop, I swear you would have thought they could be twins, she had the looks of Betty and the personality of Hyacinth Bouquet from Keeping Up Appearances and she saw herself as superior to everyone else. A Catholic lady (when it suited her), she was a Ms and had become divorced, yet she seemed to have the opinion she didn't need to work, and it was beneath her.

Once she had been married to a millionaire and had been a lady of leisure but changes in circumstance meant she now had to become independent and bring in her own income. She was another one that was menopausal and going through the change. She had an Italian blood within her and it showed, this was her fiery side, and beware anyone that went up against her!

It became apparent quite quickly that she was going to be trouble and one to watch out for. Up until I had joined the team it had just been the Manager and Madam Short Temper. The Manager just wanted a quiet life and so he didn't really stand up for himself too much, Madam Short Temper had certainly been having the biggest slice of cake and eating it. She was one of the highest paid sales assistants in the company - me joining the team meant I was a threat even though I wasn't, but she saw me that way.

Her style of selling was borderline bulling people into buying products, this was cringeworthy from very early on. I wanted to represent the business but not with that kind of attitude. Between them they taught me all they knew, both about product information and selling so I took the bits I liked and devised my own style and technique. Within a few months Madam Short Temper suddenly started to panic, I think she had written me off at first due to me being quiet and reserved. Funny how lots of people mistake being shy, and quiet as a sign of weakness! I have always seen it as a strength in people and an unspoken conversation of survival skills.

Madam Short Temper would blow hot and cold for no reason just as I had experienced with Lady Crumble, only this time on a worse scale. I didn't really understand what there was to get so angry about, she was clearly bitter and seeing herself as a victim where her home life was concerned. I have always been of the opinion it is best where possible to keep work and family life separate, don't let them cross over and overflow too much. We all had our hard hats on, on the days that she was working. Weekends would be the worst as it would be the three of us in together, I felt like I wished she had an off button, but she didn't. She would just talk, criticise and bitch about everything and everyone. One day she overstepped the mark big time...

I had been there for over a year and her menopausal outbursts where on an all-time high - think of a stroppy toddler literally throwing a rattle out of the pram because they can't get their own way, well this was her. By this time, I was becoming drained and tired. I have never had or ever wanted children, some people love them I personally don't, it's not that I don't like them I just find them hard to interact with, yet here I was with this fifty something toddler! I felt like I was the parent - it was the weirdest work experience ever.

One day I had greeted a set of customers. Madam Short Temper had this habit of thinking every customer she had ever spoken to was automatically hers - problem was the customers didn't want to deal with her, where possible they would literally lunge themselves to me. Naturally if I was going to work with them, I would be having any commission from the sales, I didn't come to work to fund Madam Short Temper's life style I had my own bills to think about. After the transaction was done, they started talking about furniture, at the time you got paid more for furniture. For example, if goods were sold at 6% commission and you sold a set for £700 you would get £42 commission on top. Not bad, and the more you sold it quickly built up to a nice littler earner - best of all you did not pay tax on commission. (I think they have since changed that format however).

I completed the transaction and the customers left happy, job done. Or so I thought, but Madam Short Temper was seething with anger and she literally looked like a bull dog chewing on a wasp! "That was my customer" she quickly piped up "they had come in four months ago!" Four months ago - they have been to sleep since then, this was ridiculous! This was starting to happen after every transaction me or the store Manager did, how were we meant to all earn a living? At no time had the customer even acknowledged Madam Short Temper, if she had spent time with someone and they had said, I would have been more than happy to pop the sale on under her code.

This however was pure greed "I'm sorry Madam Short Temper they haven't expressed any acknowledgement that you have assisted them before. They were quite happy dealing with me, they bought products that were new in the store and had just been launched. I'm afraid that was my sale, end of". She literally looked at me and screamed in my face (I kid you not) what the f***!!! this was a grown woman! I walked away in disbelief. It didn't end there.

We had a yearly diary that sat on the front desk, it had a thick red leather front cover and it was packed with all sorts, it was a big old size. It reminded me of the spell book from the film Hocus Pocus but without the eye looking at you! Anyhow, to my horror she grabbed it and launched it right at me. Yes, it sounds almost comical writing about it now, but she literally threw it across the room at me. I felt like all the flames from hell were getting thrown with it as she stood on and watched like some mad woman. Luckily it missed and stopped at my feet, this thing must have been travelling 30 mph in the air so would have knocked me clean out if it had hit my head. I decided that was it, I was literally working with a fruit loop. I remained calm... she wanted me to react, I wasn't going to, there were no words, I simply handed over my keys, got my coat and bag and walked out.

I went to my car questioning what had happened this surely wasn't normal behaviour? Yet it seemed to be the norm and my life, enough was enough! I first phoned the Area Manager and updated him and then HR. Now the problem was, no one wanted to stand up to Madam Short Temper, they knew she was a complete fruit loop, but she was also one of the top sales people within the company and these people where fueled by a world of greed and materialistic wealth. Also, this meant that Madam Short Temper was helping the bigwigs higher up to get target bonuses in their own pay cheques! "How about if we up your basic wage would that help?" Yes, it would help, but why should she get away with what I could only describe as deranged behaviour? Whereas I took it at Coopers, I was not going to take it now, so they decided what if they move me temporarily to another store.

I wasn't sure what that was going to achieve as it was just putting a plaster over an ever-growing crack. They agreed I would have a pay rise and could claim travel costs on top, this worked out to be quite a bit more, so I agreed. I really loved the job, I was good at it and I didn't want to have to keep drifting. They moved me to the Yeovil branch which was a good forty-five minutes away from Westbury, it wasn't ideal, but I was surrounded by normal people. For a while I could breathe a sigh of relief again.

Borrowed Time

I guess because I was blessed with the family I have, I've always been of the opinion you should treasure and do all you can for each other. As the true fact of the matter is, young or old, we are all on borrowed time.

Me and Paul where getting used to life in Westbury, we had been there several years by this time. On weekends he would occasionally go back and see his family in London and stay there I tended to work weekends, so it didn't matter too much to me - I wanted him to enjoy and embrace his family. The problem was there was still a huge elephant in the room... they still didn't know that Paul was gay, we were a couple and Paul was living a life as himself in Westbury. I think on some level they must have known, but people are sometimes scared to understand or learn the truth.

Paul was starting to see his family less and less, we would have talks and sometimes heated discussions. I would push for him to come clean and let them know the true world he lived in. I wasn't sure if it was because he on some level was ashamed of who he was or so scared of the reaction he might face - either way it was a firm NO. He was not ready to tell them about his other world. It was not my place to 'out' him, so life plodded on. I found this quite hard at times and it took me several years to understand, it wasn't anything personal, it was his own monkey he had to deal with.

As he was seeing his family less and less, I would often say "don't you think you should be going up to see them?", he was working early starts and his job was making him physically tired. Whilst he wanted to see them, the drive to London would tire him out quickly. "Yes, I will next week etc., etc." tended to be the replies. At the time I wasn't sure how or why, but I just kept getting an urgency in my stomach that he needed to be up there with them sooner than later.

Christmas times tended to be the worst, I would have a few days prior off work but was back in on Boxing Day and working straight through until the end of January - it's a busy time in the furniture business and when you make the most money for the year. Me and Paul would spend Christmas Day morning together, then we would go over to my parents and sister in Frome. Paul would stay till about 11.00 am then go off to see his family in London and I would spend the day with my family in Frome. I love my family, so it was a fun time, but there was and has always been a hint of bittersweet with Christmas time. This has tended to be how are Christmas times have been for the last thirteen years, not ideal but you get used to them!

Time rolled on and eventually I went back to the Trowbridge store as I knew would end up being the case. I tolerated Madam Short Temper as best as I could - I wasn't going to be pushed out of a job. Life plodded on and I made the best of what I had, but in the background, I still had this uneasy feeling lingering....

Halloween time was fast approaching - one of my favourite times of the year! Whilst a lot of people get excited for Christmas, as a child and growing up Halloween has always been my Christmas. I love the smell of the leaves in autumn and the way the wind blows not warm but not cold, almost with an air of mystic and magic about it.

I came home one evening from work, for some reason I had been having on and off chest pains. A bit unusual as I had not eaten too much that day, but it felt like a strange heartburn kind of feeling. As I got to the front door and started turning the key, a feeling of dread suddenly came over me, I wasn't sure how or why, but something felt wrong. I opened the door and found Paul sobbing on the sofa, he literally could not stop crying tears were rolling down his face.

Looking back, I feel so stupid, I knew that something bad had happened, but for whatever reason I didn't click that someone had probably passed over. It just hadn't registered with me. It took about twenty minutes before he could even control himself and speak so I could understand what had happened. He shouted out that his Mum had died suddenly by a heart attack.

This was sudden and completely out of the blue, Paul's Dad had been in poor health for some time and people had wondered how much longer he had, but his Mum was fighting fit as far as anyone knew. I comforted him the best I could, I also called my Mum who dropped everything and came over and we ended up all going back to her house. Looking back, I felt useless under the circumstances, I wanted to be there for Paul. He now had to make the journey back to London and I suggested I go with him. I was so worried, but he was adamant he would be OK and had to go alone. It was heartbreaking to see the person you love in tears with their world breaking around them but knowing that there is nothing you can do to take the hurt and pain away. Paul was very close to his Mum and I wondered how he would have the strength to get through this, I must admit I was so worried he wouldn't get through and would end up taking his own life.

For a while after time seemed to stand still, everything went quiet. Paul was plodding along but I could see in his eyes he was silently starting to drown, and it felt like no one could reach him. So many conversations coming from within, he never got the chance for his Mum to know and fully embrace him, I would now never get the opportunity to meet her, would she have been proud and loved him regardless? I was becoming increasingly worried that one day I would have someone turn up at my door saying Paul had done something silly. Little did we know there was an angel about to enter Paul's world.

Families are like a jigsaw puzzle sometimes you have all the pieces and it fits and makes an amazing, beautiful picture, however, sometimes you have pieces that are missing. This can make the picture imperfect and you must look a little harder to see the beauty within. Regardless of this, where possible please don't look back with hurts or regrets, if you are able to tell someone you love them unconditionally, do so. If you're someone who is currently at war with a family member, look at the bigger picture. Is it really worth it in the grand scheme of things? If it can be worked on and rectified, do it! Don't be someone that has to live every day for the rest of your life with that realisation that you will NEVER have the opportunity to physically talk and speak the truth to that person again.

> In my readings the amount of times family members have connected and come through with a 'sorry' and 'if only'. Other times clients are seeking the connection, and, in some cases, they are just unable to connect. It's hard as a reader to deliver that kind of message, and even harder as a recipient to receive. Don't leave it until then, free yourself from that stress and hurt. <u>Life is way too short</u>.

A Reminder to Live Each Day as if it is Your Last

Earth Angel

From time to time we have probably all experienced 'Earth Angels', these are people that get sent to us from the higher realms. They walk with us in our daily lives, they make, look and act a lot like you and I but they hold with them true beauty, healing powers and they are sent to do good, they usually have the ability to save a person. I have been blessed to have had several Earth Angels contact me, but none more important than this one...

> It often gets said by many mediums including me, the Spirit world will always try and get a message through to you, someway and somehow. I fully believe this ... if there ever was a time I might have questioned that, those doubts were put to bed at this point in my journey.

Days off have always been important to me, so I wasn't keen when people asked to change shifts. Whilst I will always help people out where possible, when they start taking it as a habit it's important to stand firm and know that its ok to say NO!

I think it was around springtime, the sun was out, and the world felt fresh and alive. I had plans to go out for the day with Mum (something we would regularly do on days off). However, I got stopped in my tracks this particular day, by my phone ringing from an 'unknown number' (probably the only reason I answered it at the time).

It was Madam Short Temper 'was there any chance I could come in and cover her shift?' The Manager was on holiday at the time (although that would not stop her phoning him). "It's not really convenient I have made plans" was my response, anyone else I had no problem changing shift for, but with this lady I felt I owed her nothing. As she was pleading, I suddenly had an overwhelming feeling I needed to be there.

Reluctantly I agreed, "you are helping me out of a huge hole" came the reply, I wasn't interested in what she had to say, and I wasn't doing it for her for that matter. I remember it was on a Wednesday, the quietest day of the week "Could you put any sales on my code for any comebacks"? was the final request. There was no 'thank you' for giving up my time with Mum. I said "If they make it clear they have seen you"! and with that I put the phone down and headed on in. On Wednesdays it was always worth bringing in a book or magazine to read, often the top drawer behind the desk was full of Madam Short Tempers woman's magazines, so I would flick through them and do the crosswords and word search. Nothing much was happening in the bed shop on this particular day, so I decided to keep myself active. A good spring clean was in order, I dusted, hoovered and made the showroom sparkle.

I think it was approaching early afternoon when a lady and her husband came in for a wander. I didn't want to let on this was the first person I had seen all day! The great thing about being in alone was that you didn't have to worry about Madam Short Temper pestering them. So, I told them I was about and if they needed me to let me know. The lady and gentleman where mature, mid-fifties I would have said. The lady was thin with a cream suit jacket, blouse and skirt, blonde hair in a bob style and she wore glasses. The gentleman was a little taller, balding on top with nice jumper and smart trousers. Like a lot of husbands that clearly didn't want to be there he went wandering off downstairs for a browse whilst the lady carried on looking.

Without being pushy, I asked how she was getting on and then we started talking about all things bed related. She started to explain they needed a king size divan pocket sprung fairly firm. We started looking in the pocket spring section and I talked her through the various spring counts and what the benefits would be etc. Suddenly, she just stopped dead in her tracks and looked at me, this seemed a little odd and was not the usual way a customer would respond.

She then proceeded to tell me "Oh, I have to tell you something but it's not standard procedure." 'What was she on about?', I was thinking, my first thought was 'great I've given up a day off and now I'm stuck with a crazy customer!' She then explained that she was a spiritual medium. I hadn't ever had any experience with this before, I loved watching Most Haunted and Colin Fry's Sixth Sense but that was as far as it went!

She explained she had a lady with me and started to describe her and how she passed, without saying anything I knew who it was. She then said I was a messenger for someone else and this was a Mum for someone close to me, a partner. She then went on to say she loves her son, your partner, very much. She doesn't care what he is she just loves him unconditionally. She then started describing my Grandad and the way he had passed, she is one of the very few mediums to have given an accurate account on how he passed over.

A mix of feelings came over me, the hairs on my arms and neck were going goosey but I wasn't scared, I felt a little like a huge weight had been lifted, I felt calm and at peace but wanted to know more. She then explained my time here was coming to an end, and that I currently wasn't happy with work. She saw me doing a small stint on stage in some sort of performance. She also said I would be working for a rival competitor on a higher salary, she laughed out loud and said she kept seeing me dressed in drag. Nobody in my work life knew about a little part time adventure I had been exploring on and off.

I was a part time Cher Drag Queen Impersonator (more about this later), the plan was to go full time with that. She then said I will have a bit of fun with that and earn a few pennies, but it will end abruptly. She then went on to tell me I would then be ready to do my real work. 'Real work?' I thought, my Cher impersonating was at the full front of my mind, it was the main thing I wanted to do. She explained I was a medium and already aware and working with spirit on some level. I had had a few experiences but a medium I was not, I found that a bit laughable as I just did not see it. She then went on to tell me I would be a full time medium and doing public demonstrations and eventually stage work!

She then explained she is not meant to just read randomly for people but felt it might be the only chance for Paul's mum to come forward. She explained she was doing a demonstration at a place in Westbury called The Shining Light Centre and if we were free to pop along. I had never heard of it even though we had been living in Westbury for some time.

With that her partner came back up the stairs, looking less than impressed she had been chatting for half an hour or so and off she went as quickly as she came in. I felt both happy yet confused, I didn't like the idea of not doing the Cher stuff long term, but I choose to dismiss that quickly. I was happier that Paul's Mum had stepped forward, clearly, she knew we were a couple, seemed OK with everything and just wanted to remember a mother's love for her son.

I phoned Paul from the business line straight away, he didn't seem convinced! He got quite angry and snappy with me, "Who was this lady? How dare she talk about his Mum!" came the reply and "why are you working on a day off!" A feeling of panic came over me, but I calmed him down and explained. First, I told him about the panic phone call and covering Madam Short Temper's shift. Paul has always looked for the trickery in everything, he is one of those people - he has to see it first hand to believe. I then explained to him "Don't you think it's weird I'm not even meant to be in today?" Divine timing played its part once more. I then started telling him what she had said, while no one knows about your Cher thing, and your Grandad etc. I said, "why don't we see this lady tonight at a demo thing whatever that was, then you can make up your own mind first hand?"

He agreed he wanted answers from this lady. I felt really worried! What if she wouldn't be able to do it again, and what if it had all been some sort of hoax. I knew in my heart it was true, this wasn't some cold reading this was personal details coming out. There was no way she would know, backed up by the fact I should never have been in that day.

We went into a small hall with plastic chairs put out, there was also comfy high back chairs scattered around the edge. We sat there and got a few looks, clearly a lot of people knew each other. A Scottish lady came up to us and introduced herself as Jean and asked had we been to this before. We explained we were new and told her what had happened, she just smiled and said enjoy...

The lady I had seen in the bed shop came out of a side room onto the front area dressed in a little black jacket with purple shirt, and black pencil skirt, she seemed nervous. Please don't let me down I thought. This was a huge step for Paul coming to something like that, and I was just trusting in the higher powers that all would be ok.

She delivered her first message and we got an idea how she worked. We had sat at the back so probably won't get picked on, we thought we will be quite safe. With that she looked down at Paul and bang, bang she was off.

'S****' I thought not only was she accurate she was fast. The message is now all a bit of a blur, but I was captured by what she was coming out with. She mentioned a small photo Paul had recently put in a silver frame, she described the frame and photo and where it was in our home. There was so much being fired at him he had no choice but to believe, I turned to Paul, he literally couldn't talk he was in floods of tears. He managed to gasp the word "Wow" out, Jean came over with some tissues, and the lady next to him gave him a hug. It was a lot to take in for him. She then did me a brief message at the end and explained how we had met earlier on in the bed shop, much to everyone's amusement.

I have not mentioned who this medium is purely, as she is as a rule, quite a discreet person with her own spiritual work. For purposes of the book I will simple refer to her as an Earth Angel. And she was, she really was. When the demonstration had finished, we looked at each other in complete shock, at the time Paul was smoking and needed a puff after all that. I joined him outside as also wanted some air, the medium followed us out and said do you mind if I puff and chat with you. She started saying a few personal things about our relationship at the time but said we were solid and would last despite outside influences. She again referred to Paul - his mum loved him regardless of what his sexuality was. I honestly don't think there are enough words to describe or put across just how amazing this experience had been. This Earth Angel had in her own way saved both me but more importantly Paul. I knew by what had been said there was no way he could have questioned it.

When we got home, I phoned Mum wanting to fill her in on everything that happened but for some reason whether it was a delayed effect I'm not sure, I just burst into tears and explained I would call her back. I think the realization of what had happened hit me, and it was overwhelming. Me and Paul spend that whole night in bed just chatting and coming to the awakened sense that there is indeed an afterlife or spirit world. I had always known this anyway, but had I had any reservations they were all quickly put to bed. I truly feel blessed that my Earth Angel was able to connect the two worlds and pass these messages on, I know it has given Paul restored hope and a new way of viewing the world. It's an experience so powerful it will stay within our hearts forever.

Despite the message being so strong, there was a few things I struggled to accept. The Cher business being short lived? Working for a rival company? the mediumship stuff I would be doing? I put those parts down to being wrong, I dismissed them quickly ... How wrong I would end up being ...

Can You See the Angel Within the Trees? Taken Whilst Out Walking the Dog

Bad Omen

About two months later I did indeed start a new job as the spiritual medium said I would. It felt great to be leaving Madam Short Temper in the past, and all the baggage that went with it, I decided I didn't want any more menopausal woman causing problems. From now on it was straight forward enjoying life, or so I hoped.

Well... looking back there was a possible warning sign. The interview for this new company had gone well, the only downside was that I had to drive to the Cheltenham store to have the interview. My car at the time was a newish one that I had treated myself to, taking out finance, it was a black Rover Streetwise. Not to everyone's taste but I really loved it. The interview went well, I knew my products, so it was straightforward, they could see I had hit my targets etc. but told me the targets would be slightly more. However, I was ready for a new challenge 'no problem' I thought, they offered me the job on the spot and I only had two give a week's notice so that was that. As the medium had said I was now working for the rival bed company on higher pay.

On the drive back home, things didn't quite go to plan. I was on a huge roundabout just off the retail park that led you back onto the motorway. As I was heading through the lights they suddenly changed. I was a bit stuck, if I stopped, I would be halfway across the road so the safest thing to do was carry on to the motorway lane.

As I was doing so, a driver that could see me crossing their pathway, suddenly drove straight into the passenger side of my car. Without really knowing what had happened I suddenly felt the full force of the car hitting mine, my car spun around, and I was now facing the wrong way in the road! Cars were literally coming at me from all angles. Within minutes an Ambulance and Police team were called, by some miracle I got out without any scratch on me, the driver of the other car claimed he had severe whiplash although to all onlookers he seemed fine.

After some questioning by the police they checked over my vehicle. The back door on the passenger side was complete crimpled in, however they said it would be OK to drive home. I was so shaken I literally felt I couldn't move let alone drive, I phoned Paul and then my parents to explain what had happened and I let the traffic calm down to allow the roads to become a little quieter. Whilst driving home I felt a mix of emotions, I also felt annoyed with the psychic lady, how had she not seen and pre-warned me this would happen. I had a very ignorant approach back then and I didn't realise it was out of her control, spirit would show what they needed to, if she was never shown it, how could she pass it on?

Admittedly I was a bit arrogant back then to what I didn't yet fully understand. I also clearly felt that some kind of guardian angel had been with me. I survived without one scratch, I felt like the higher realms where protecting me that day.

Life in the new bed shop was pretty good, I was in a team with two other older gentleman and for a time life was gentle again. I didn't have any crazy energy. Whilst everyone there seemed to be fueled by money there wasn't any drama to deal with in the same way I had with Madam Short Temper.

The extra money coming in was a welcome bonus and I was able to put it to good use - or so I thought at the time. Looking back now I cringe a little and whilst I _have_ done the maths, let's just say we are talking thousands of pounds spent…

No, not saving for a mortgage or anything of that nature…

Cue big wigs, false eyelashes and all that sparkles…

Step to the side Mitch… CHER is in the house!

If I Could Turn Back Time

As I mentioned earlier, I had a separate job outside of my normal work. It wasn't until the latter years I let work colleagues know about my alter ego, about a year before I stopped performing. I was a part time Cher drag queen impersonator. I would do my drag act at gay bars, birthday parties, charity events and anywhere else that would have me perform.

It's very important that I let you know what drag meant for me. The art of drag is the illusion of becoming a character and taking on a role. I loved the magic, the transformation and shape shifting from a male to a female. For me drag was always about performance and creating a piece of art, and the chance to play a character and escape the everyday world for a time. (Just so we are clear, there was never anything sexual or questioning of wanting to become a female, this is something altogether different).

Cher was my idol and I had grown up with her music and her energy being in my life from a very young age. When I was living in London, I would often see beautiful drag queens caked in makeup, taking on the role of an alternative persona. I quickly got the bug and behind the scenes I spent large amounts of time practicing how to use makeup and studying the movements and mannerisms of Cher.

I had friends that were already impersonators and doing it full time and earning good money. So, I thought 'yes' why not? I would like to do some of that'. It never really entered my head if I could do it or when, it was more a case of this will happen, and for a time it did, and I loved it...!

The problem when you impersonate someone like Cher is you don't just have a couple of looks to master. There are literally hundreds of different outfits and wigs one needs to get. I started researching where to get my costumes made. A lot of drag queens I noticed made their own, some were stunning but a lot of them looked cheap and nasty. Their makeup and stage act were fabulous, but the costumes let the whole illusion down. I decided if it was going to be Cher, I needed to have the best of what I could get, this meant not only costumes but wigs also... I researched local costume makers and some from afar, no one seemed to really be ticking the boxes.

Finally, I struck gold and found a costume maker, KikoAmore in America, who designed outfits for a whole catalog of drag impersonators, brilliant I thought! We had the conversations about what I needed and in no time at all, he started to work his magic needle and thread. The first outfit I felt I needed to have was the iconic Turn Back Time body stocking covered in rhinestones and crystals, this baby set me back £400!!! But to be Cher this was the main outfit I needed. Next, I looked at wigs, again getting them custom made, £200 later I had some decent Cher hair. I spent hundreds on makeup, tights, fake breasts, hip, and side butt padding to achieve the female shape I needed, I also had an array of boots and heels and whole manner of other accessories.

I know what you're thinking, 'more money than sense', even as I write I'm cringing but at that time in my life all my spare money would go on creating the show. The way I used to justify it to myself was... a show would pay anywhere between £100 to £600 depending on venue, requirements etc. So, I used to think of it as a couple of big shows and its paid for itself, looking back now I really wished I had spent the money more wisely and invested it for a mortgage or rainy day, however hindsight is a wonderful thing.

I also sometimes feel I was harsh and quite cold towards Paul at this moment in my life, yet through all the out of control spending Paul supported me. I think he hoped deep down I could be successful as he has always wanted me to do well and be happy. But he is a lot more grounded with certain things, so I think he also knew before I did, that this would be doomed or short lived.

My show consisted of me singing live and lip-syncing to certain songs, sometimes gay bars preferred the lip-syncing. Looking back now I sometimes think I was a little ahead of my time, drag has become extremely popular in the UK with the huge success of the Ru Paul's Drag Race TV series. However, when I was performing it wasn't as popular over here and was more established in America.

It's often questioned if I could sing as Cher? I think this is part of the fun when you do drag, you don't have to be able to sound 100% like the person, you can get away with a lot more. I certainly had good and bad days, sometimes I could just about 'blag' my way through certain songs, other times it was clear my voice was not where it needed to be. This was the main difference with all those other impersonators, they didn't have the best costumes, but they could all sing, they had real talent, which at the time I thought I had too… but looking back now I know I didn't. I had talent in the sense of my look, if it was just based on being a lookalike I did look like Cher when done up. Even when I lip-synced the whole show was perfect, but my own singing left a lot to be desired, and in time would become my downfall.

Nevertheless, I wasn't going to let a small technicality hold me back - Cher had launched what most have been her seventh farewell tour - this meant new costumes that needed replicating. One of the outfits a lot of other acts on the circuit were starting to recreate was the famous snow queen opening coat. This baby was pure perfection, I decided that I wanted to try and use a UK based costume maker for this one. I just happened to stumble across a London based costume maker that made a lot of Lily Savage's costumes, that was it, I was sold. I sent a message to James Andrew Maciver. He has created outfits for numerous celebrities and been involved with costumes in West End shows and many other high-end productions.

I knew he was the one I needed to work with on this outfit. He too also had a vision for making sure things were as true as possible to the original. I sent him an email and numerous conversations later we were in business… This costume was one of my all-time favourites and the most expensive I have spent on a piece, it cost me £600 but I still feel it was money well spent. This piece had so much detail to it, a lot of work went into recreating the original Bob Mackie design. It was perfect and gave my show an extra piece of wow! £600 is a lot to be worn for one song but I know I had one of the best coats within the Cher tribute world.

In-between doing my day job, I had some fun performing at various venues and events. One of my all-time favourite events was a charity show in Cardiff where I was the last to perform of the evening. It was a brilliant night with a host of all different types of act, I felt I stole the show a little, as soon as I came on stage the place went wild… I decided to do a mixed medley of songs and came out in the snow queen coat with dry ice smoke everywhere on stage… I sang all the songs live that night and my whole section of the night was brilliant.

The last song I performed was Believe and everyone was on their feet dancing, singing and laughing. I'm not sure if everyone thought I was good as Cher or if some found it more of a comedy act, but I didn't care, everyone was loving it. When the show was finished, I had so many people asking if I would perform at certain venues etc. so, I couldn't have been that bad…

Thinking back and reminiscing over these times makes me smile. It was a strange but interesting adventure and I feel blessed to have performed for those that enjoyed my shows.

Little did I know back then that the winds of change where coming for me, and in the distance a storm was brewing…

Cher Extravaganza

Empathic

Time rolled on and it felt like there was a change coming... One thing I have always been aware of with retail work is often people end up staying there. Certainly, for me anyway, the work colleagues often had broken dreams and found themselves working in retail, very few people set out to do that, more a case of floating. I was finding as time went on that I was becoming extremely empathic, more so than I had ever felt before, being empathic can be good and bad, when working in an aggressive sales environment it's not always good.

I was starting to feel a huge shift within myself. I used to love the buzz and pressure and challenge of hitting targets but it's like I suddenly woke up and I was starting to dislike the world I was in, certain behaviours were slowly starting to disagree and not sit well with me at all.

With all my retail jobs people seemed to come and go. I found this was a theme to that happened quickly right back from the days of Coopers, therefore I find it hard to have real friends. I have many acquaintances and people that feel like they are a friend, but my circle of people has always been pretty small. I am fortunate for I love my own company, so I don't feel I need too many people in my world.

I started finding that as soon as someone stepped over that invisible barrier from being an acquaintance to a friend, they seemed to end up leaving me behind and go off on new adventures. At first, this took me time to get my head around - I didn't like it when someone started moving on, as I felt I was once again being left behind in the distance.

One day I had a bit of a lightbulb moment and started to realise what was happening. Like a moth to a flame these people where gravitating towards me and what they felt to be a friendship was more of a healing journey. They always seemed to have a degree of baggage or drama and never understood why I seemed calmer and at peace with the world. I used to advise these people on what I would do in the situations they found themselves in, looking back now it was almost like I was healing these people through my words and voice. The ones that choose to act upon it suddenly seemed to take control of their lives, then a short while later they felt it was OK to leave mine.

I was starting to feel like a traveller or stranger in the world that I knew. But I also realised that this pattern or cycle of energy was playing out time and time again - the characters were different, but the story was always the same.

Years later when I fully embraced my spiritual work, I have been able to channel this type of energy in a different way. I can spot the signs a lot easier and usually these types of people, end up becoming clients that are in need of healing.

> A 'healer' is not someone that you go to FOR healing. A healer is someone that triggers within you, your own ability to heal yourself - *Author unknown*

The Show Must Go On... Or Not

Life carried on, but I started to feel I was outgrowing the places I was in and started to feel stuck with work. There were a lot of new area Managers being brought into the company and masculine dominant energy was suffocating my world. They usually had a life span of between four to five months, just as you felt you got into a routine with one, they would leave the business and a new one would then come in. All full of bright ideas and thinking they knew best - but full of bullshit, ego and broken promises. The sales job was easy, but these newbies were starting to up the pressure cooker of energy. Suddenly I felt like I had gone from working in a bed shop to being on Dragons Den or The Apprentice - this was not what I signed up for, it was getting tiresome and I wanted out!

I still craved the magic of the stage; my shows were on and off and I continued to perform as and when I was able to. I got a booking for a show bar venue in Worthing, the owner was a transvestite called Lady Lush – a slender queen, with a long blonde wig, long fake nails and she wore a skimpy number. Whilst she looked quite feminine when she spoke, she had the voice of a bricklayer. I packed my Cher gear into the car and off we went, Paul came with me to this one, so he drove. I was excited to be venturing further afield and somewhere new but there was also a feeling of disappointment. I couldn't put my finger on it, but something just didn't feel quite right, I was unsure why.

We arrived at the venue - it was not quite as it was advertised from the website, it looked like a lovely show bar from the photos in an OK location. When we arrived, it was clear we were in a rough part of Worthing, the sky and buildings all looked grey and forgotten. Me and Paul both looked at each other a little unsure of what to think, 'I'm sure it will be fine inside' I thought. We went in and Lady Lush greeted us with a warm welcome. She was dressed in thigh high silver boots, and a red velvet corset with black leather hot pants. Her aura was enchanting there was something about her... she had you in a sort of spell like trance, and you just couldn't take your eyes off her.

As we arrived around 5.00 pm we had a drink as I wasn't due to perform until 8.00 pm. Lady Lush seemed lovely, but we noticed the clientele was not the normal for a bar of this type - rough and ready builders were in there getting wasted, and an otherwise mixed bag of people. One or two gay couples where dotted around. Usually gay venues have a very relaxed warm, gentle feeling, and as a rule cater for the LGBT community, however the community seemed to be lacking here, this just felt broken and a mismatch of energy.

I set up my stage area and did a quick sound check, all seemed fine with no problems. I then set up my costume area behind the stage curtains - in the show I had between five to six quick costume changes. Lady Lush took me to what I thought was going to be my dressing room area, to start applying my Cher face, the dressing room ended up being a very greasy kitchen area. I wasn't very impressed, but it was this or the gents' toilets. I felt this was the best of the two options... as I'm writing this now there were a lot of warning signs. But I was professional and wanted to create and deliver my show to the best of my ability, I had been booked in good faith and needed to deliver the goods.

The makeup took anywhere from an hour to an hour and a half to do. Sometimes fake eyelashes would go on easy other times I would be wrestling to get them to sit how I wanted. Layers of foundation and other drag secrets were used to create the look of Cher. When I was happy with everything, Lady Lush came in "oh darling you look fabulous it's like we have Cher in the house!" she was making all the right noises. She commented on how she loved my outfits and said they were the best replicas she has ever seen. She ushered me to a side curtain, so I was now behind the main stage curtain, I put on my snow queen coat and looked in the mirror. The intro music started up, dry smoke started to fill the stage, I didn't feel nervous when I was in character, I almost felt like I was Cher and Mitch was turned off for a while.

Lady Lush, introduced me "Please welcome to the stage Mitch As Cher…." That was it - show time! I came out and the place went wild… I performed the first four songs and the crowd seemed to be loving it. People where dancing and singing along and from what I could see everyone was enjoying the night. Then… probably one of the worst moments of my life happened… I think it would be any performer's nightmare…

I went off stage for my first costume change of the night, I had an instrumental section of music giving me just three minutes to change into my next number. Cher is known for amazingly quick costume changes so this was something I had practiced and worked on. I was pretty much in the second outfit, all was going fine I thought, then suddenly the music stopped. Shit! I thought 'has the track skipped?' - no it hadn't. Suddenly Lady Lush was on the stage and demanded I come out, she sounded really angry. I grabbed my next wig but in sheer hurry I could feel it was slanted and not on properly.

As I walked back onto the stage, she suddenly gave me the biggest dressing down of my life. "Your costumes are lovely, you look amazing, but you cannot sing…" Was I hearing this right? Suddenly the audience that had been dancing along with me just seconds prior where now booing, hissing and screaming abuse at me. "Get off the stage!" they were screaming, you would have thought I was the wicked queen in a pantomime the way the audience was carrying on. Lady Lush went on to say, "You need to have a good long look in the mirror and decide what it is you are, as a performer you are not!"

Was I hearing this right? I was being asked to stop my show and go? I was waiting for there to be a catch or expecting the likes of Ant and Dec to appear from their "Saturday Night Take Away" show and say it's all a big hoax. Sadly, it wasn't… I wasn't sure whether to laugh or cry, it's one of the most bizarre experiences I have been put through.

I suddenly went into autopilot mode; the job now was to get out of there as quickly as possible within one piece. It's very, very scary to have a whole audience of about a hundred people turn on you, and literally spitting abuse in your face. I gathered up my costumes and everything was being literally shoved in the car as quickly as possible. We had everything except my stage backdrop…

Lady Lush said she wasn't paying us for the night, Paul started having a go and getting nasty! She ended up giving us £30 petrol money, so we could at least get home - we ended up leaving the backdrop there, Paul wanted to fight for me, but I just wanted to go. I felt in utter and complete shock... what the hell had just happened? Paul had already had a few drinks so was over the limit, so I had to drive in full Cher slap. Tears were rolling down my face, but I didn't cry.

I thought to myself 'was I really as bad as she had made me out to be?'. The audience seemed to be loving it, but it's surprising how quickly someone can turn on you when there is a ringleader. I thought about all the other shows I had done, I never had one bad reaction.

People sometimes ask me how I felt about this experience. It's very hard to describe, at the time I wasn't upset, more insulted that my act had been cut short. I was also really annoyed the whole time my wig had been sitting on me slanted, and off centre.

The next day I had some messages from people that had been at the show, they were saying how much they had enjoyed it and were shocked it was cut short. They also said they thought it might be jealousy on Lady Lush's part and to not give up. That was just it the experience left me broken, luckily I didn't have any more bookings only enquires so I decided to remove my website and closed all my Cher business pages down with immediate effect. The experience brought on an extreme depression and anxiety.

The Cher outfits were all packed away I didn't want to look at them, let alone wear them - they literally made me feel sick to even see them! Everything I had been working hard for seemed to have come crashing down around me. I suddenly remembered the words the spiritual medium had said years before. "You will have a career on stage, but it will come to an abrupt end, you will then go on to do your real work..."

I thought about this, had she seen I was going to be booed off stage? Again, feelings of anger, upset and frustration washed over me.

The following months I felt I was in a dark place of emotional grieving, I lost all focus on everything, the Cher shows had kept me sane. It got so bad I didn't even want to listen to Cher for a while as the music just brought the whole experience back to the full front of my mind.

Divine timing was about to strike once more...

My Opening Show Number – Who Knew Four Songs In My Life Would Never Be The Same Again?

Enchanted Tarot

I felt that I was walking the world with a compass that was spinning out of control and guiding me down a dark pathway. Everything at that time felt like it was going wrong, and I just felt in a constant state of numbness. Around four months after the Cher disaster, my place of work announced they were closing half their stores and the Frome store that I had been working in was on the list to close. Part of me saw this as an opportunity for a new adventure, but because I was still in a low place myself this just added to the pressure.

Luckily, I wasn't out of work for long - the area Manager at the time, an Asian man known as KK phoned me up, and asked "would you work in the Trowbridge store?" I had been Assistant Manager in Frome but would be a salesperson again if I took on the new role. This was a complete comfort blanket for me, I knew the job inside out, so it made sense and I agreed. The only issue was the Manageress of the Trowbridge store was another menopausal, middle aged, ego hungry, psychic vampire. Fueled by money and all things materialistic and by all accounts a trouble maker. For the purposes of the book I will call her Lady Double Trouble. The healer in me always tries to see the good in someone, so I kept an open mind and tried not to judge Lady Double Trouble despite all the hearsay and gossip.

I settled into the new store and work seemed to continue as it had always done before. I was left on my own quite a lot in the Trowbridge store and this didn't bother me as I enjoyed my own company. It's often said that when the student is ready the teacher will appear...

One day when I was pottering around putting stock away, a lady came in with what I assumed was her husband. They started looking around and I told them if they needed any I was about. The lady walked past a new range of beds we had, these were top end products, one of which was called 'Enchantment'. They both started laughing which I thought was a bit odd. The lady saw that I clocked them laughing and called me over, she started to introduce herself as Annette and explained she was a medium and tarot reader amongst other things, and her business was called Enchanted Tarot, so it suddenly made sense as to why they had been laughing amongst themselves.

We got chatting and she suddenly felt the presence of a gentleman... ('oh no here we go again' I thought). She described my other Grandad who had only been gone around a year or so at that time, she told me that he was OK and well. She then went on to say there was extreme sadness in my heart, and I felt like I was in a world that I didn't serve any more. She explained I was a medium, a tarot reader, and a spiritual soul. But she could also see I was hanging on to resentments and hurts that were blocking and stopping my progression and moving forward. She told me about a new group she was putting together, it was a meditation circle to de-stress and heal the past and when the time was right, we might do a bit of psychic development.

I wasn't so worried about the development part. But I was feeling stressed, over emotional and almost here in person but not in self. I felt very dead behind the eyes and to the world at that time, so I decided at £5 per session there was nothing to lose and possible lots to gain. I agreed and said I would see her on Wednesday evening.

She asked, "have you ever done Tarot?", I hadn't done anything like that, so I decided to have a one to one reading with her. I felt at a place in my life where I literally didn't know where I was or what I should be doing. The reading was insightful and touched on lots of things I had been going through, it gave me food for thought but I was still a little unsure as to where I should be. The cards were all pointing to a more spiritual pathway and walk of life, but in order to have this something would have to go - I felt at peace and uplifted but still unsure of where I should be within the world.

A Deck of Cards That Would Change My World Forever

Still the Mind

Wednesday came and I went along to the first meditation circle, I was full of nervous energy and anxiety and a level of excitement I had no idea what to really expect. Annette welcomed us into her home and we made our way to the back garden, she had a lovely log cabin area with roaring fire, beautiful Indian tapestries and other mystical pieces decorated in the place we used to meditate. There was a group of around five of us, I was the only male in the group, the others were all more mature ladies - this was fine as I always felt more at ease with female energy. Annette explained how the circle would run and conducted the first meditation, I didn't feel a great deal at first apart from feeling able to process information in my head. I kept thinking 'was I doing it right?' - she then asked what we had experienced and gave us a little summary of what may have been happening. It always seemed to make sense.

As time went on, I started to really enjoy my Wednesday meditations with Annette. I found myself really looking forward to them and being mid-week, it helped to reduce and release the stress from work. I was also starting to allow the process of meditation to work for me and with me, I wasn't fighting or questioning it anymore, I was going with the flow, and being open to whatever experience was shown.

She started to bring in the psychic development side as she had said she would. By now we were all quite a nice little group, and there was good banter between us. She handed us each an angel card and we had to then all swap and read for each other. Some of the ladies felt overwhelmed with nerves and couldn't do it, I also felt nervous and unsure what I was meant to say or do, Annette explained to just trust and go with what you feel, sense or see. With that one of the ladies handed me her card with a gentle smile across her face I felt like she really needed some sort of guidance. I looked at the card which I can still remember now said 'release...' - with that words just flowed, and I gave her a message of about ten minutes long.

Afterwards I thought 'where the hell did that all come from?'. The lady in the group said it made complete sense and tears of joy were in her eyes, I think I had given her massive validation about something without being fully aware. When it was time to leave Annette asked me to stay on and wanted a quiet word, she asked whether I had done any form of development work before and I said I had not. I told her about some of the weird goings on from my younger days but said that was all. She explained she was running a tarot workshop and felt if I was interested, I might be quite good - there was no need to make a hasty decision, she told me to have a think about it and let her know next week...

I thought about it on the way home, I had only ever had one experience with Tarot and that was when Annette first used the cards with her reading, so I wasn't overly sure of their full power. I spoke to Paul about it that evening and explained about the course, he thought it might be a good idea, although he felt I should be careful and make sure I wasn't getting involved with anything dark. I must laugh a little at this point as looking back we were both very ignorant to what we simply didn't fully understand.

I decided I needed a new focus and a distraction from the Cher saga. Whilst this was still painful it wasn't having quite the hold on me that it once did, and through the meditation I was slowly doing my healing work and making my peace with that.

Wednesday appeared once more and I said to Annette I felt the time was right to learn the Tarot cards...

Meditating and Pondering Life (Check Out My Dreads Here!)

Time to Learn

It was the day of the Tarot workshop, again I was nervous and excited, full of wonder as to what might await me. The group was made up of two other ladies and me all from the meditation circle. The course started, and Annette started going through the basics of Tarot, I had been slightly unaware of how many cards were included in a Tarot deck. Suddenly I felt slightly overwhelmed with having to learn the meanings to seventy-eight different cards! Annette's approach to learning was good, and the kind of style I liked, both practical information and very hands on - getting thrown in at the deep end.

Lunchtime came, and I felt like I was buzzing and a little overwhelmed with all the information that had been going on and I had taken in. The afternoon was about putting the theory into practice, we did a lovely meditation beforehand to reground and earth ourselves. Then it was time for us to have a go at using the cards in a reading, I was extremely nervous as were the two other ladies. To add to the pressure Annette let us use her reading room and we were only allowed in one at a time. She explained we were all going to read for each other.

I read for the first lady and I was a little unsure of what to think, whilst she said it was good, I felt it was pretty poor. I then went on to read for Annette, again she said it was a strong reading and would get stronger with time, but she could take or understand the information being given.

Finally, I had to read for the last lady of the group a lovely lady called Kim. I started reading Kim's cards and it was very weird as I felt like the cards were starting to vibrate and talk to me. I had not had this happen with the previous two readings, I started to see and say what I was feeling, getting and sensing from the cards. Kim said it was all very relevant but was very much about past experience. One thing Annette had always taught me from the start was if I got a 'no' to challenge the information - was it a 'no' or was it simply being miscommunicated in some way?

I felt into the energy and said I feel this is a current situation or something coming in within the next two weeks. Kim looked on and was a little defensive saying "No, no its simple already happened" and with that dismissed the situation. I said to Annette after how the feeling made me feel weird, as it didn't feel past related, and I didn't feel upset but a bit annoyed that Kim wouldn't budge with that. Annette smiled and just said well done and let's see how this unfolds. She told me "Remember we cannot force information on to someone, it could be you are correct, but Kim is not ready to acknowledge this." I decided to admit defeat and left it at that.

Annette draw the course to an end and said something that ended up being so true. Tarot is a tool like anything else. If you nurture and work with the energy it will in return work for you, if you forget and don't work with it, your links will become broken and patchy. She then went on to say one of you in this group will go on to work full time with Tarot. One of you will dip in and out as and when, and the other will put away your cards in a drawer and do nothing with the cards after this workshop. That was exactly what ended up happening…

The weeks rolled on and I started to feel alive again, Tarot had awoken something within my soul that I hadn't realised was there before and I spent the coming months learning, connecting and working with my deck of cards whenever possible. As Annette had said the readings and information started to become clearer and stronger than ever before.

About a month past and we met up on our weekly meditation night. Kim said, "Before we start Annette, I owe Mitch a massive apology". I felt really confused as to my knowledge she hadn't done anything bad that I was aware of. She went on to say, "I completely dismissed your reading without being open to what you were saying", but it turned out everything I had predicted within the cards had come to light and was accurate.

Kim also said, "Had I listened I could have saved myself some unneeded drama". I don't like to say, "I told you so", but me and Annette looked at each other and it was like we were talking telepathically. We both said in thought 'See, told you so'. It certainly would prove to be the first of many times to trust the inner voice and feelings more so than anything else.

Something I have had to learn and figure out – always trust your gut feeling even if you have no idea why. Nine times out of ten there is always a reason, and your psychic body is trying to help you and prewarn you.

Putting My Trust in the Universe

Lady Double Trouble

I feel at this stage in the story I could write a whole book on Lady Double Trouble... but don't worry I'm not going to! If you remember, Lady Double Trouble was middle aged perhaps late forties early fifties and of a catholic religion (when it suited her). She was short and quite round, she was also partially deaf and had hearing aids in both ears - this did by no means affect her abilities in any way, shape or form.

Lady Double Trouble was a very determined lady, on the face of things she seemed really lovely, and she could be. But... like others I had already encountered she had a fire, different from others I had experienced but equally hot and unpredictable at times. I had been warned of Lady Double Trouble's ways before I signed up to work under her wing. I am however a firm believer in not getting caught up in gossip and seeing things first hand in their true light.

The months rolled by and me and Lady Double Trouble formed a nice working relationship, as I had been in the business a lot longer than her, I already had very good knowledge for how things worked. She liked the fact that I was self-sufficient and got on with jobs without being asked, she was surprised how well the team seemed to respond to me. She couldn't understand how I could them to do tasks, yet when she asked nothing got done.

Respect - quite simply treat someone as you wish to be treated. This had always been the way I was with coworkers, often managers have a habit of feeling superior and would try and throw their titles around. Whilst Lady Double Trouble did not do that with me personally, I saw from an early stage, that she did that with others in the team.

Time went on and things were OK, people seemed shocked that I was able to handle Lady Double Trouble and we actually had a nice working relationship for a time. But like others I had worked with she seemed to have two personalities - some days she would be lovely, would even want to mother me, we would laugh and joke, and the day was a pleasant one. However, at times she would come in and be really short-tempered and would take it out on the team. I really struggle to work with people of this nature, I like consistent energy and to know where I stand with someone at all times.

Lady Double Trouble was ruled by greed, power, and ego, this sadly was her downfall and as time went on, she started to change how she was. She didn't seem to like it that all members of the team had respect and were for the most part working in harmony. She seemed to get very caught up in her title and would constantly remind us that she was the Manageress of this store and what she had to say was law! She also started to play the team off each other and would spread little white lies, the sad thing is on some level she actually believed the lies she told. The team was strong without her and we all quickly started to see her game. Little dramas flared up over the coming months and I tried to keep myself as neutral as possible as I came to work to earn money, not get caught up in child's play.

She started to phone me when she had days off wanting an overview of how the day had gone and I would tell her if it was a good or bad sales day - she would get really annoyed if a day had been slow. As time went on, she then started ringing me after hours wanting to talk, at first I answered the calls thinking maybe it was business related but she seemed to be offloading all of her problems onto me, both work and personal home life. The healer and empath in me thought perhaps she was lonely and needed a friend to talk to, but this carried on and was getting to the point of being a daily routine.

I would finish work at 6.00 pm drive home, and get back around 6.25 pm, she would then be ringing anytime from 6.30 pm onwards. If I didn't answer straightaway, she would continue ringing, leave voicemails, send texts and demand I contact her back that evening. This was getting a joke, I wasn't paid nearly enough to be dealing with this sort of behaviour. The working relationship had taken a toxic turn, and I was becoming extremely drained.

The phone calls didn't seem to happen just on her days off, I may have spent a whole day working with her and still when I got home, she would ring. This was not normal behaviour for a Store Manager and a team member, I felt like I was being stalked and my personal time was being invaded. It also started causing problems with those around me, my relationship with my partner, family and friends. The phone calls were never short, anywhere from twenty minutes to an hour and half - half the time it felt like Lady Double Trouble was talking rubbish just for the sake of talking. What I noticed was there was a pattern forming, with all different topics she went on about she was making out how she was the victim, and how hard done by she had been, and how the world seemed out to get her.

> Our actions and inputs affect our physical world. The mind is very much like a magnet - what we think we become. If you send out negative energy, that's what you will attract back. If you send out positive energy you will attract this back within your world.

I felt like an emotional sponge soaking up all this rubbish from Lady Double Trouble, she also was extremely competitive. The store was at times the highest performer within the South West area, obliviously being ranked number one as a Manager she would have had an additional bonus paid to her. The problem was she made no secret about saying how she was the top salesperson within the team, that was the problem! As a Manager she was only meant to be doing twenty to thirty per cent of the selling, her team should be doing the rest. She started becoming so pushy and aggressive on the sales floor and determined to be the top salesperson, that no one else was getting a look in.

Mondays started to become a day I dreaded, we had to do a personal weekly one to one review report where you would talk over with the Manager how the previous week had been. Did you hit your sales target? If not, why? How many KPIs did you achieve? How many orders did you get delivered that week? How much was done on credit and so on…

Lady Double Trouble took great pleasure in ripping each of the team members apart. It was always a double-edged sword - if you hit your sales target, you would rarely get green boxes on everything else such as KPIs (which are add-ons like pillows, soft bedding, headboards etc.). My weekly target would be around £9,000 per week (more in the busier months) and if you hit your sales target you would be told off for lack of KPIs. If you hit all the KPIs but missed the sales target you would be questioned intensely on why this had happened - it was very rare to hit everything across the board.

Sales Target means – 'A goal set for a salesperson or department to be measured in revenue or units sold for a specific time. Setting up sales targets help keep you and your sales team focused on achieving your goals.' It is a goalpost to aim for to hit the target, but naturally there will be times that it's missed. What had always been a brief quick overview in the past, was like being on The Apprentice or Dragon's Den with Lady Double Trouble. She took this review process extremely seriously, usually making the team feel like dead wood and rubbish at our jobs before we had even started the day.

I tried extremely hard to let this process go over my head as Lady Double Trouble had a way of making you feel worthless in seconds. She decided that since I had been going to Annette for meditation that this was the reason my sales had dropped and suffered, the reality was the economy had been hit hard by the recession and people were struggling to stay afloat. Often people would come in wanting credit only to be declined, everyone was suffering.

I certainly was not prepared to have to justify to Lady Double Trouble what I did outside of working time, she had no business knowing and it didn't affect my working world in any way, shape or form - if anything, the meditation kept me grounded and helped me survive longer there than I would have done.

Lady Double Trouble continued to set the team up to fail at every given opportunity. The team decided to put in a joint grievance - this way we hoped we would get our voice back. The problem with direct sales retail is that everyone earns money along the chain, so whilst the Area Managers knew Lady Double Trouble was hard work, they were all hitting their bonuses through her, so it was in their own interests to keep her sweet.

A meeting was called, and we all laid our cards on the table, I used this opportunity to mention the constant phone calls, at which the Area Manager at the time was shocked. He made it clear that had to stop with immediate effect, (they didn't stop altogether but significantly reduced). The Area Manager was concerned that the whole sales team was ready to just call time and quit, he did however use a lot of emotional projection, blackmail and mind games to try to make us think our own behaviour had broken down the relationship with Lady Double Trouble. This of course was not the reality, but he would be earning a nice little bonus of around £500 to £1,000 through her per month - money is the real cause of all evil within the world of sales.

He did, however, decide that it was not fair for me to be doing the work of an Assistant Manager and not getting paid for it. He felt I was not cut out to be an Assistant Manager despite me doing it in the Frome branch with no issues for the last 4 years! So, it was decided that the Assistant Manager of Swindon store (who we will call Lord Pretty Boy) was appointed to work with Lady Double Trouble until further notice. Lady Double Trouble was not happy and had her nose firmly placed out of joint. Over the coming month she put on her best behaviour and tried to get on with us all, and for a time the turbulent waters settled and stilled once more…

Lord Pretty Boy

Lord Pretty Boy was a very bouncy young man, in his early twenties, he was definitely a bit of a 'Jack the lad'. He was quite nice looking and easy on the eye, but he thought himself to be a lot more handsome than he actually was - beauty is only in the eye of the beholder, the soul is where the true beauty lies. Whilst he had a charm, he also talked for the most part complete bullshit - he looked down on the team and thought he was better than the rest, another person consumed with ego and self-importance.

When he came into the store, he very quickly started making himself at home. When I shook his hand, I felt the presence of spirit coming in close around me showing me a black snake wrapping around him like his body was a tree. Whilst I was learning how to understand what spirit where showing me, it was crystal clear this was a warning of some kind. This took me a back a little, he saw me gasp and said "don't worry I get that reaction a lot" then "I've heard you're gay… I'm cool with that as long as you keep it to yourself." I smiled to myself 'yes darling, I'm gay not blind…' –

I love how straight men think when they around a gay person we are automatically going to jump them. I said "sorry to disappoint you I'm in a happy twelve-year relationship thank you." He seemed completely shocked that a gay person could be in a happy long-term relationship. He then started asking me 101 questions on the subject and how the average life span of his relationships had been around a year as he gets bored quick - that says it all I thought!

The other thing I noticed early on is that Lord Pretty Boy liked to be quite close when talking, he also had really bad breath which surprised me, for someone who the whole time he had been in the store had been checking himself out in every mirror of each furniture room set that was on display! A mix of stale lager, smoke, and a McDonald's meal, not very charming at all, a welcome gift of a packet of mints will be required I thought to myself.

Despite his arrogance and bad breath, I wanted to try and give him the benefit of the doubt. He went off with Lady Double Trouble for a team meeting, they were complete yin and yang energy, so it would be interesting to see what unfolded. Lady Double Trouble quickly made it clear that Lord Pretty Boy needed to back her on all managerial decisions. Lord Pretty Boy quickly said he would back the best decision for the whole team not what was best for her, this seemed to come as a shock to her system. At last someone that was as hot tempered as Lady Double Trouble and was willing to stand up and fight back.

The first week came and went and the store became a place of Zen and calming energy. Lord Pretty Boy seemed quite hard to talk to at times, the subjects seemed very limited to football, girls and getting pissed - I wasn't interested in any of that. On one Wednesday I asked, "Do you mind if it's quiet if I take back some hours?" The company owed me a lot of overtime that they didn't want to pay so we all said we would take it back in time off. Wednesday is a good day for me to finish early so I asked.

Suddenly Lord Pretty Boy become quite intrigued and asked me, "Oh, why is that do you go to a book club or something?". He started laughing at his own joke thinking he was a laugh a minute, so I just rolled my eyes and smiled, "no I go to a mediumship night on Wednesday". I didn't - I went to a mediation and development evening with Annette, but for some reason it came out as mediumship.

Suddenly, he wanted to ask a million and one questions, the awkward silence was filled with him wanting to know everything about my other life. I also told him a little about my witchcraft but made it clear the others didn't know about it, it wasn't that I was ashamed of being a witch, quite the opposite but... I didn't feel they were the right people to be sharing such personal details with.

The weeks rolled on and me and Lord Pretty Boy started to form a bond, but I kept getting a 'spinning wheel' within my stomach and a feeling to go very careful, but the friendship continued. I also told him that I did Tarot (and I had been doing free readings).

Straightaway he wanted me to do him a reading and practice on him, we were heading into autumn time which was always quieter, and we didn't see many customers during the week, so I brought my cards in explaining I wasn't very good but will see what I can do.

I did him a spread of cards and the information just started flowing… I knew by his reaction he was very sceptical about the whole thing, but by the end he was in shock. "How do you know all that just from some cards?". I said how I had done a workshop and had been practicing ever since, he said he understood the reading, I was just looking to his left side when I saw quite clearly next to him an older gentleman standing there. I didn't say anything at first, but he could see from my change of expression that I was looking at someone. Lord Pretty Boy said, "is there a ghost next to me?" he said he felt extremely cold on the side I was looking at. I told him "I'm not sure, well there is but I don't know who they are".

I had told Lord Pretty Boy I didn't really do mediumship which was true, I didn't, I had only practiced once or twice in Annette's healing hut. He asked me what the person looked like, so I described the gentleman as best as I could and said he looks almost like something from a negative. I could see him, but I couldn't, but I could - it was very hard to put into words. Lord Pretty Boy said, "what does he want?" with that the spirit gentleman showed me one birthday candle so I said, "he is showing me a candle, I think there's an important date of some kind coming up". Lord Pretty Boy said he understood and with that the spirit gentleman blew the candle out and vanished as quickly as he had stepped in.

Lord Pretty Boy explained it was his Grandad and today was his birthday, he had been asking for a sign and thought maybe he might come in during the card reading. I thought he was going to laugh it all off and call it all 'hocus pocus' but to my surprise he seemed genuinely impressed. He wanted me to keep everything discussed in the reading private which was a no brainer. But he did smile and tell me he thought I should be doing mediumship as well.

I wondered about that for a time as it had been in the back of my mind. I went on and did more free Tarot readings around my working hours, but no more spirits came in. Stick with the cards I thought.

How wrong I would turn out to be…

The Shining Light

I continued going to Annette's meditation evenings and I felt like I was becoming more at peace with the world around me. The whole Cher experience didn't upset or affect me like it once had, and I also found the meditations were making me calmer within myself, everyday things seemed easier to deal with.

Before we went into Annette's on this one Wednesday some of the girls talked about 'The Shining Light Centre' in Westbury and asked me whether I been before and if I wanted to go. The only time I had gone there was about four years prior when the lovely medium came into to see me and I had the message from Paul's Mum, but it had been on and off in the back of my mind for a time. We spoke openly to Annette about it, it was, after all the place that she herself developed and made sense of her gifts. She gave us all some friendly, sound advice, and we made a plan to go to the development night the following Monday.

Monday came, and we all went into the hall, Jean greeted us, and we explained we were new to this. Jean asked what our level of experience was, complete beginner and we all said, 'terrified and nervous'! I explained how we go to Annette's meditation evenings on a Wednesday and that I personally do Tarot. She looked at me and said, "I know you", I reminded her about when me and my partner came to the demo all those years ago. She just smiled and said, "well it's taken you four years but you're here now".

The chairs were all put out into a circle and we sat down and started to introduce ourselves, everyone was lovely and warm. After a small mediation Jean split the group up, we went with the beginners and did some work with a pendulum, none of us had done this before. The whole evening was magical we all felt this was what we needed alongside the meditations from Annette.

The weeks went on and very quickly Jean split our little group up, two of us went into the platform group where you learn to work with direct spirit, the rest stayed in the beginners' group. Without warning Jean suddenly called my name "Mitch you're up first". "Um oh I'm not sure about that" but before I had a chance to decline, I was in front of a small group of around seven or eight people. 'Hmmm help' I was thinking I had no idea what I was doing or what they thought was going to happen. Jean whispered in my ear "trust and let your spirit team in to work with you". With that, information started flowing, I described the spirit I was seeing and the person I felt drawn to. I gave what I thought was a load of random waffle but to my complete surprise the lady said it made complete sense, I was really taken aback.

Jean then told me I would stay in this group for a few weeks. It was a strange feeling, on the one hand it felt completely natural and like this was what I was destined to do. On the other hand, I felt like a complete fraud, 'who was I thinking I could channel spirit?'. I convinced myself it must just be a fluke or the lady telling me what I wanted to here.

On the following week once more Jean put me in her group and when my turn came to do platform again, I was riddled with nerves. She placed a clear quartz crystal in my palms and said I should look at getting something to hold, as it will help calm me and relax my hands when I was on platform. Again, information started flowing from nowhere, this time I had a young boy come through, a couple who was there said it made complete sense and had tears of joy in their eyes. I found this hard to watch as I didn't want to upset anyone, although they reassured me it was happy tears of validation.

Maybe, just maybe I had finally found my calling…

The weeks continued, and I made sure whenever possible I was at the circle. The bed shop stayed open until 8.00 pm one in five nights and those where the only times I couldn't attend. It was a really important time in my spiritual journey, so I needed to be there as much as possible. I was mixing with souls that were completely on my wavelength of understanding and I didn't need to be careful with what I said or censor my conversations.

Anything to do with the spirit world and the hidden realms was up for discussion and I felt like I was 'coming home' and for the first time was in a circle of people that didn't judge me. Everyone just accepted each other's colours in their truest form. The room was full of unconditional love, a place for everyone to learn share knowledge, heal, and grow together.

This feeling was something I had never experienced within my working world before and it's a feeling that will stay within my heart forever.

I stayed and committed to the circle for a good year and half to two years… but whilst my spiritual world was blossoming there was a snake in the grass that was about to expose itself.

An Energy Portrait by Angela Ferreria – Magic Paintings

In the Frame

Springtime was in the air and the world was starting to awaken from its winter slumber. There was an excitement as plants were beginning to re-bud, blossom and bloom – there was the smell of spring magic, but I kept getting an overwhelming feeling of doom, I wasn't sure why?

Things were going OK within my working world, Lady Double Trouble and Lord Pretty Boy would often disagree about the way things should be run and whilst this was draining on one hand it took the focus off me and the team, so I was happy to keep my head down and let the battle of egos continue.

Lord Pretty Boy had booked a weekend off to go to Cornwall with his girlfriend and see a friend. We both worked the Friday shift together before he was leaving for his weekend holiday around 3.30 pm. A customer came in that day at around 3.15 pm and pay the balance on an order (the company had a policy where once cash reached £1000 it was expected to be banked that day unless you were working alone). Lord Pretty Boy processed the transaction in the normal way and I asked if he was going to the bank before he left. He replied, "Do you mind if I leave it as I really want to get away sharp to Cornwall?" I wasn't too worried and didn't think much of it, after all it would just get banked on Monday along with the rest of the weekend's takings.

We agreed to leave it as had been done numerous times before and I told him to go off and enjoy his weekend. He left ready for holiday adventures in Cornwall and he wasn't coming back until Tuesday the following week, so it was a nice needed break for him.

Lady Double Trouble, myself and the part-timer buckled down to a weekend of selling and hitting targets, it was nice to have the old team back working together. Lord Pretty Boy was OK to work with, but everything seemed to be a drama with him. The lifestyle he had was really worlds away from mine, and I often cringed at what he found funny and what he got up to. Sometimes being an old soul on young shoulders means you just do not 'get' the youth of today's world, no matter how hard you try.

Sunday morning arrived. It was company procedure to count the cash every morning and input the amount onto the computer system that was linked up to head office. The cash tin was the most secure I had ever seen, hidden in a vault, then with various locks! The room itself was locked and you could only gain entry via the door keypad which had a code that had to be changed monthly on a five-week cycle. I think even the greatest lockpicker would struggle to gain entry!

As I was first in, I counted the cash and found everything as it should be! No additional money was taken on the Saturday, Sundays however were a different story as at the weekend, customers often popped in on a Sunday to make balance payments which could be tricky if we were all busy with customers. The only person whom didn't have a set of keys was the part-timer, so they had to constantly ask to use our keys when handling cash, this was tricky if you were already half way through processing an order.

3.30 pm approached and the team was all buzzed up, we had hit our weekly store target and it happened to be a week when we all hit our personal targets too. This was great as Lady Double Trouble would be happy for the coming days ahead. 3.30 pm until 5.00 pm tended to be the graveyard shift where you would see the odd customer coming in killing time but rarely purchase. The shop was quiet, so we often used this time to start the admin, get all the performance reviews out the way and get ourselves ahead of the game. We got the cash from the safe in the vault - £2000 was taken that Sunday, giving a balance of £3000 to bank on Monday and we had our separate fixed till float that always had to be £40.

Lady Double Trouble counted the money and we all agreed we were happy it was present and correct, we made the bank book up ready for the next day, as it helped to make things quicker and easier. Monday was delivery day so if the banking was prepared and ready it meant we kept ahead of the game.

We all celebrated at having a good weekend, locked the store and put the alarm code in, a weird loud buzzer sound would go off allowing three minutes to shut the door and lock up - we all said goodbye and made our way to cars. By this time there were usually only our three cars plus a few 'boy racers' on the far side of the car park having a KFC or McDonalds as the rest of the retail park had more sense and had closed at 4.00 pm. Lady Double Trouble drove out first, followed by myself and then the part-timer who lived in Frome so at the first roundabout he shot behind me and took his exit. There were three more roundabouts that I followed Lady Double Trouble on, then we parted company on the third and she took a left off to Chippenham, and I went straight across past the petrol garage on the right heading to Westbury.

As we parted company, she waved her hand, today was a good day I thought. It's hard to explain if you have never worked in direct sales before, but it can be at times an emotional experience. When you have a good day you feel buzzed, alive, happy with the world and on an off day, or if you missed out on your target this can send you into a negative space. That day I was buzzing, and the magic of spring seemed to really lift everyone up around me.

I feel the events that followed, that I'm about to share with you were really a test from the spirit world. "A test?" you might say. Spirit, as I have learned, test us from time to time. I was awakening to my higher self on the one hand and this experience highlighted a life lesson or two to me which was that not everybody works from the heart. We can give someone the opportunity and accept them on face value, but this does not always make them genuine or good. At the time I knew it was a test, but it was a hard lesson to learn. Whilst I know there is light and dark within the world, I try to be of good character and judgement and I've always been taught to treat a person with respect and as you wish to be treated. Perhaps I got caught up in being a bit naive - the healer in me always wanted to see the good in someone.

The next Monday morning I arrived at work around 8.30 am as usual (although I was only paid from 9.00 am, it was easier to arrive early even if I didn't get paid for it). The roads where always rammed, risking leaving even five minutes later could result in complete gridlock or getting in late.

On this morning something weird happened as I went to put my key in the lock, I suddenly saw the black snake that I had originally seen on Lord Pretty Boy. This did make me jump I have to say, as I was still half asleep and whilst I'm not scared of snakes, in equal measure I don't really have any desire to be touching them. I thought perhaps I was just overtired, I tried to put the key in again and all was normal. I put in my alarm code, and silenced the alarm buzzer, relocked the door and unlocked the fire exit I then flicked the kettle on and went to the toilet which was pretty much my normal routine.

I made my first brew then went to open the till and set up the order pad online for the day ahead. What happened next was sadly a case of human error on my part, I don't regret what happened as I feel it had to. I pulled out the bank book and started to enter the information into the online till - standard practice was to count the money before inputting it into the computer. I wondered what would be wrong, bearing in mind we all counted the money last night, so I entered the amount that we wrote down and submitted the entry. It wasn't that I was trying to be lazy or cut corners, I just felt there was no reason for anything to be astray. How wrong I would end up being…

Lady Double Trouble came in bright eyed and happy, still buzzing from the weekend's victory. She had a morning brew and we started to plan our day, around fifteen minutes later we thought it best to get the banking done. Before we took it down, we would always recount the money so I got it all together and started counting. I kept recounting because something was wrong… Lady Double Trouble looked at me with concern and asked, "What's the matter?". After counting numerous times, we appeared to be down by £1000!!! "That cannot be" Lady Double Trouble said pointed out we all counted the money last night before leaving. Lady Double Trouble recounted the money herself and sure enough we _were_ down £1000. I told her I input the money before counting it and I expected her to blow her lid and throw me a fireball from hell but to my surprise she stayed calm. Whilst I should have double-checked it, she understood entirely why I went ahead and input it onto the system.

"Let's not panic" she said, "let's retrace our steps and check we haven't dropped it en route". We searched the small vault but there was nothing to be seen or found… Neither of us could understand how the money could be gone, what was weirder - why would they just take £1,000? It didn't make sense, if you were going to rob the place you would take the lot, but someone has been in and counted out £1000 only. We have had at times between £9,000 and £10,000 in cash in peak periods.

I knew I hadn't taken the money and I knew Lady Double Trouble and the part-timer hadn't either...

We had no choice but to inform the Area Manager and the Banking and IT Departments. Lady Double Trouble as a rule was hot on admin and knew her legal rights so said to me, "whatever happens next make sure you get a paper trail of everything". The only other person with a set of keys was Lord Pretty Boy but he was down in Cornwall - or was he? I told Lady Double Trouble he knew there was £1000 in the safe. I asked in my thoughts for my spirit guides, angels and helpers to help, I had never felt so worried in all my life, I knew I was innocent but also how it looked, with the added problem of not counting the cash before inputting onto the system.

The Area Manager at the time had a low tolerance for Lady Double Trouble as he had become increasingly difficult and annoyed with her challenging stuff. We explained what had happened and his reaction wasn't so calm. He was furious and gave me a load of verbal abuse, I tried to let this wash over me as best as I could, but the empath in me wanting to crumble and cry. 'Do not show him tears' I thought, and I held it together. He sent the alarm company as they were the only people able to access an activity. This was the other weird thing, had an intruder gained entry the alarms would have gone off, but they didn't - everything was correct.

The engineer came out quickly and started to access the alarm key pad control, he saw we had all left at 5.05 pm on Sunday afternoon and that someone had turned the alarm off at 5.15 pm. The Area Manager demanded to know what code they had used, the engineer read out the code that belonged to Lady Double Trouble - this was impossible as I had followed her home, whilst she did my head in at times I could not stay quiet and see an innocent person take the blame for something they had not done. I saw red and started fighting back saying to the Area Manager "Don't you think it's all a bit suspicious that this happens when Lord Pretty Boy is away, the only other key holder?". The very fact I brought his name up annoyed the Area Manager even more, he then felt that perhaps Lady Double Trouble and myself were both involved together.

Feelings of panic, injustice and anger came over me and I found it extremely insulting that I had worked for the company for nearing ten years and this was the thanks I got! What an insult to think I would steal £1000 when there has been the opportunity for a lot, lot more.

I'm the sort of person that doesn't even take a grape out from a bunch they are buying for fear that a hidden camera might be watching in a supermarket! That was the other problem with the business all the CCTV was fake so next to useless.

I felt like my world was unravelling fast, I suddenly could see there was absolutely no loyalty. I was merely another cog in a very large spinning wheel and a number easily replaceable. I wanted to just throw my keys in and quit on the spot but of course I couldn't. I was very much now a suspect and 'in the frame', the task in hand was to now clear my name!

All or Nothing

With immediate effect myself and Lady Double Trouble had to hand in our keys, and we were both suspended pending further investigation and we were to have no contact with the store or each other. The only contact would be from the Area Manager or HR Department, Lady Double Trouble grabbed me and hugged me as we collected our coats and bags from the staffroom and whispered in my ear, "follow the process, remember paper trail everything". With that we were both escorted to our cars and drove home.

As I was driving the journey home and thinking everything over in my head, I wasn't crying but gentle tears were flowing from my eyes. I wasn't worried about the job so much, it was the fact that I had been so loyal to everyone around me. Often giving up personal time for the needs of the company at a cost to myself. There was no loyalty, or any attempt made to hear my side of the story.

I decided to drive up to the White Horse in Westbury and clear my head, I parked up and walked over to a bench and I just watched the world down below me. I thought to myself everyone whizzing around at a hundred miles an hour, trying to please and impress companies and job roles.

I looked at the birds flying and dancing through the sky, such wing span, such freedom, no limitations, no demands from the physical world. As I was making sense of life a few experiences happened. Whilst I couldn't tell you who was with me, someone was sitting next to me from the spirit world on the bench. Perhaps it was a loved one, perhaps it was a spirit guide, perhaps it was just my higher self? I will never truly know. But I felt the energy and presence of a gentleman. I asked in thought, 'why am I being put through this? Why am I in this mess?' The voice answered in thought 'you have always had the wings like the birds in the sky, you have chosen to put yourself here, keep yourself limited from flying high and gaining purpose'.

I didn't understand what my purpose was at all. "Think on" the gentleman said and with that his energy vanished and I was alone once more on the bench. Suddenly and from nowhere another car came into the car park. The occupants were blasting out music, at first all I could hear was the base, then I started to hear the words. Of all the songs it could be it was Cher - All or Nothing… this was the first real time I had heard any Cher songs since my experience on stage. I have always received hidden messages through songs, just one of several ways my spirit team work with me.

This was way too coincidental to be anything else. The song continued… "I don't wanna run, but I can't walk out. Who do you think you're fooling? Who do you think you're fooling? Baby it's All or Nothing Now". I suddenly felt the vibration and power from the music. I reconnected with what I loved originally about Cher's music, her voice and the true healing energy when you listen carefully to the words. I felt energised but more than that, it didn't feel painful to listen to - the healing journey around that experience felt complete.

As I listened, I kept seeing Lord Pretty Boys face, "Who do you think your fooling? Who do you think your fooling" I knew it was him, but I just had to prove it. With that my phone started ringing, it was an unknown number, I had a strong feeling I needed to answer.

It was only Lord Pretty Boy - despite not being allowed to contact me or Lady Double Trouble he started going on before I even fully registered it was him. All he kept saying was "I know you haven't done it and I will make sure this gets resolved". I tried to work out if his energy was sincere or not, I just couldn't tell. I think perhaps he wanted to frame Lady Double Trouble but through my actions I had implicated myself.

I will never fully know - one thing was certain he was carrying on this masquerade of still being in Cornwall on holiday. I felt like I had a black snake next to me on the bench. I kept my responses to one-word answers and tried to let him just talk, I didn't want to give him any more evidence to use against me. As he ended the call something weird happened, the black snake I was being shown, started to shed its skin. Hmm I knew this was a sign, in Tarot a skin being shed means a time of change, growth and transformation. I suddenly understood what I needed to do…

Cher Opening Number and the All or Nothing Song in My Cher Show

Justice

I left the calm and stillness of the bench at the White Horse, slowly made my way back to the car and drove home. I decided to get full clarity on the position I was in I needed to consult my Tarot cards. (*You may laugh at this... whilst some people in this situation, may have sort advice from a Citizens Advice office, or legal action, for me I knew the cards would give direction and outcome*).

Although I was a reader and had been doing Tarot for a good few years now, as a rule I never read for myself. Some people don't read for themselves purely as they question the information being given and wonder if their own thoughts are influencing the reading too much. For me this was not the reason why I didn't read for myself, quite the opposite in fact. In the early days when I had read for myself Tarot always told me what I needed to know, it was very direct, blunt and to the point. Almost too accurate (if there can be such a thing) and I found as time went on I didn't always want to know and was happy just plodding along.

However, this was a time of emergency and I needed quick, definite answers so I knocked the cards three times, started to shuffle the deck, sending my thoughts and questions into the cards. I pulled the first card and asked to be shown the situation I was in... I had The Tower... this card made perfect sense to me.

I continued and asked the cards for Lord Pretty Boys input... The Moon card literally threw itself at me out of the deck. The Moon is a warning card when shown, suggesting not all is as it may seem on the surface. The Moon was hiding two faces. As I looked and read deeper in with this card, it started vibrating and almost felt boiling hot to touch. I was again shown the black snake within the card, but this time it struck as if it was going to bite me. I knew 110% that he had done this, I just now needed to prove it was a setup.

I asked for what would happen and await me at the interview meeting... The Five of Wands appeared. This worried me a little as this card refers to conflict, but it was also reminding me as it was Wands and not Swords, to stay grounded, earthed and not allow the energy of others to silence my truth - I knew the interview process was going to be emotional, mentally tough and draining from this card. I asked the cards various other questions to help make sense and fit all the puzzle pieces back together. What I love about Tarot is when used correctly it can really help to give accurate advice, the cards were telling me the clearest of stories as I knew they would.

I requested a final card to be shown to me as a conclusion or overall message. Two cards immediately fell out from the deck... Justice and The Star, I knew that all was going to be OK, The Justice card was showing me a fight but the truth would be exposed, bringing balance and restoring order, The Star was a time of awakening, shining my true light and purpose out into the world.

As I studied The Star card, I suddenly was reminded of the words the medium told me all those years before. "You will have a time on stage, but it will come to an abrupt end, you will then go on to do your real work". I knew from the power of the reading that this was my calling, like the star a being of light. I also knew that to fully embrace this new age of being, something would have to go.

Before I could explore that fully, it was time to clear my name...

Good Always Triumphs Over Evil

Seeker of Truth

Three days later with the reading still fresh within my head, it was time to start the investigation interview process. I drove into the car park, my anxiety and nerves where at an all-time high, the way my anxiety and nerves was flaring up it must have looked like I was guilty from the start. Why was I so nervous? I hadn't done anything wrong, I was an innocent party as was Lady Double Trouble, yet here we were both in the frame, having to fight to clear our names…

    I walked in at my agreed time, as I entered the store the part-timer and Lord Pretty Boy where both on shift. I was already briefed I wasn't allowed to talk to them, just go straight to the staffroom where the Head Office team would be ready to conduct the interview. The part-timer gave me a gentle smile, I looked at Lord Pretty Boy, I didn't look at him with my physical eyes but from my third eye and I could feel an energy of guilt written all over him, but also arrogance. He clearly thought this was already done, in the bag, that he had pulled off a massive scam and won. I sat down, and the interview process began.

The way I was interviewed was like something you see on the TV, the whole process lasted about two hours and I felt drained and burnt out as the cards suggested I would. I didn't get angry, shout or raise my voice despite the interviewers at times getting very frustrated with me. They tried to use a lot of protection and mind games in the hope of tripping me up. They didn't like it that I wouldn't back down and they concluded that me and Lady Double Trouble must be in it together. The part-timer had confirmed to them he saw us both leave on the first roundabout, but as he turned off to Frome he said he couldn't say either way what may or may not have happened next.

I asked the team about the petrol garage, they have a camera that points onto the furthest side which should show the roundabout and we would have both been seen on camera. Despite putting this request forward, they refused to even investigate it. I was shocked out how they were handling this situation, this wasn't some reality programme this was real life, and peoples' livelihoods would be at risk including my own livelihood!

They called time on the meeting... as I left it was Lady Double Trouble's turn... we both had had no contact with each other or seen each other since we turned our keys in. We shot each other a look of respect and telepathically I kept hearing the words "Seeker of Truth". Lady Double Trouble was different to me, she would have already sought legal advice and be making sure she built up a file to take the company to court. As we looked at each other I knew that was it, our working relationship would be over whatever way our stories end.

I was told I would hear news over the coming days. About four days rolled by – it was a horrible time. Whilst I was free in that time to do as pleased, I couldn't focus on anything. I thought about looking for alternative jobs, but every time I tried to focus I just couldn't, I spent the days sleeping most of the time. My body had taken on too much emotional distress and I felt like everything I had been through was catching up with me. The sleep was needed to almost heal and recharge my soul like a battery.

Friday morning came, and I still hadn't heard anything, so I decided to have a morning coffee in my back garden. I sat down at my little bistro chair set I had and looked up at the sky, as I looked up, I saw the most beautiful white feather within the clouds. A feeling of peace, rest and stillness washed over me but more than that, I felt all the white noise in my head stop for a few minutes.

I had a feeling something good was about to happen. I carried on drinking my morning brew, looked once more at the clouds, the feather had disappeared and the clouds where just swirling once more within the sky.

Suddenly my phone rang, I took a deep breath and answered, it was a member of Head Office. "Good news we would like to now end your suspension period and welcome you back to work". I didn't understand what was happening, a few days ago I was told I was number one suspect. The team member told me they had found evidence that showed Lord Pretty Boy had taken the money and he had resigned with immediate effect, but there would be legal action. Lady Double Trouble had also sadly been dismissed from the business with immediate effect for not overseeing her duty of care to the store. She will be taking legal action against you I thought for unfair dismissal – she did just that and won!

The team member continued "We don't expect you to come in this weekend, take it off and then be ready for Monday, business as usual, just pop in at some point over the weekend to collect your keys and new alarm code". With that he ended the call, there was no 'sorry' at any stage for what had happened.

Part of me was relieved it was over, and I felt like Karma had kicked Lord Pretty Boy's ass. But I was also upset that Lady Double Trouble had to leave in the way she did., she was indeed the seeker of truth. It turned out that whilst I was having my meeting, she was having a meeting of her own over in the restaurant that was directly opposite the bed shop. She was very friendly with the Manager there and asked if she could take a look at their CCTV footage in doing so, she saw all of our cars leave the retail park but then Lord Pretty Boy walked into shot dressed in his uniform. Wasn't he meant to be in Cornwall on holiday with his girlfriend?

When I questioned that story in my interview, they said they had evidence he was where he had said. It transpired that a friend of his manipulated an iPhone to show he was in Cornwall at such time, even though he was never there. The footage saw him enter the store using the alarm code, anyone else around at the time would have thought he was going back in to the store and had possibly forgotten something as he was in uniform.

Once I learned the truth, it made sense to why I had seen the black snake so much within his energy. I felt a bit shocked and saddened that he had clearly planned this for some time. Was it to take Lady Double Trouble out? Did he do it for the money? Had he planned to get rid of us both? I will never fully know and don't really care.

The experience taught me that despite trying your best with someone, you are only one person and can only do so much. The healer in me tried numerous times to give Lord Pretty Boy the benefit of the doubt. Whilst my psychic body was screaming at me to tread with care.

> I have learned that energy doesn't lie… it has no reason to. When you get a gut feeling around a person or situation, trust it. You may not know why initially it might take days, weeks or even months, but… your psychic body is warning you for a reason. There is always a reason.

People have since questioned why I didn't use magic or witchcraft. Sometimes however powerful magic can be it isn't the answer to everything. Sometimes we must go through the pain and frustration of the physical world. Had I not gone through that experience, I would have stayed stuck in a place and time I had outgrown. Whilst it caused pain and upset, it also highlighted and showed me that I was surviving life rather than living it – changes needed to happen, I should be living life… and enjoying it like the birds flying free in the sky…

The Feather in the Sky Gifted from Spirit

Trust

New doorways were ready to open, but I decided to carry on for a little longer in the bed shop. I knew I needed to move forward but I didn't feel ready to just up sticks and leave. I had nothing to leave for and felt I needed to at least start looking for new jobs. There was a real bitterness in the air, so I decided from here on in I was just going to do my work, I was no longer willing to go the extra mile for people as there was clearly no loyalty or regard for me as a person. I knew I was just a number and a cog within a continually expanding wheel.

With both Lady Trouble Maker and Lord Pretty Boy now gone, it was down to me at the part-timer to keep the store afloat. The Area Manager was also coming to the end of his life span and so for a time we had acting Area Managers. This made things a lot easier as we were left alone to get on with the work in hand. I found myself beginning to chill out and not be so uptight or get too worried about the work as I had done in the past.

Because of this I was making sense of the world around me and I felt the spirit world coming in a lot stronger than they had ever done before. Often as I was chatting to customers, I could feel the energy of their loved ones from the spirit world pushing forward, wanting me to pass on messages of evidence and reassurance. Whilst I knew this was wrong and not standard code of conduct I also knew this may be my one and only chance to let these people know their loved ones where safe.

Despite trying to ignore the spirit world, I was no longer able to turn them on and off as I had once done. I was reminded that when you develop your energy moves to a higher vibration - I was stepping into my truth and purpose whether I felt ready or not.

I decided to let people know but in as gentle way as possible, I would often say "so outside of work I am a spiritual medium, I have someone linking in with me, is it OK to pass on the information". Nine times out of ten, the customers were open to hearing what I had to say. I only ever had one person that did not wish to know and so I didn't pursue that conversation. It was a magical feeling, almost seeing the weight of the world leave people as they knew there was no way for me to know what I was coming out with.

I felt so torn I knew that this could not continue, either I would get rumbled at some stage by the bigwigs at Head Office, or I would say something to someone that wasn't ready to hear it and land myself in hot water. I tried where ever possible to stick to the task in hand and sell them a bed!

I had gained a lot of experience whilst developing at The Shining Light and with Annette's meditation nights. Annette approached me one meditation evening and asked did I wish to join her at a spiritual church doing an evening demonstration of mediumship. At first, I wondered if this was a trick or joke, she had heard I was getting quite good and felt like the time was now to move forward. She said she wouldn't put me forward if she didn't feel I was ready and that it was only a small place and I'd be fine. I was so unsure and felt the nerves coming back with force but before I had time to process a response, my mouth had already done it for me and came out with the words... "yes..."

Oh no! ... that was it I had just committed myself and didn't feel I could back out. The only time I had done anything with an audience before was when I was booted off stage and I wasn't sure I was ready to put myself in that line of fire again. But before I could change my mind... "Brilliant!" she said, "I will see you on Sunday and meet you there". That was it, I was booked in and doing it.

Over the coming days I felt sick with nerves. I was excited on the one hand as I knew I could do platform, as I had been developing for a time by now at The Shining Light but the biggest crowd there around seven or eight people. Whilst Annette assured me the group was small, I knew it would be bigger than that so I kept worrying the whole time - I did not want a repeat of the Cher days.

On Sunday I was a bag of nerves, a friend of mine named Dawn who sold spiritual gifts was also coming to run a little stall at the back and gave myself and Paul a lift. I was panicking the whole way there and they tried their best to calm me down and put my mind at ease. We drove into the little car park of Corston Church.

The first thing I needed was the toilet and to settle my stomach, when I had the first of about ten toilet breaks before I was due on I went to find Annette, she was with the lady that ran the centre, Jan. Jan was a beautiful soul, she gave me a warm hug and I could feel she was powerful but also had a gentle nature. "You will be fine" she said with a beautiful healing smile. She whispered in my ear "spirit have been wanting to work with you for quite some time already".

I knew on some level this was true, she went on to say nerves are a good thing, they keep you grounded, and it shows you're working from the place of love without ego. The only thing you need to do is send out the love to your spirit team and allow them to come in and trust whatever they give you.

The doors started to open, and people started making their way in. Me and Annette went into the small kitchen area and did a mini meditation and got into the right headspace, she could see I was white with nerves, but told me she didn't have any bad feelings and I would be fine. I had my last toilet stop, and then it was time to go and sit on the platform. As I sat there I realised there were a lot more people than I had expected, around thirty-five to forty. "Ooo it's a good turn out tonight" Jan smiled and said to me, "someone must have heard you were coming". She took my hand and gave it a gentle squeeze - cold hands but warm heart!

Jan introduced the evening and we sent out some healing, we then sang a hymn although I muttered through trying to steady the nerves. Annette then introduced me and herself and explained how the night would work. I thought I was going to do maybe one or two messages, but she explained we would go back and forth meaning we would have done around thirty-five minutes each in total! I didn't have time to 'chicken out' now. Annette delivered the first message and it all made sense. It was then my turn - as I was getting up from my seat, I took a deep breath and said in thought to my spirit guides, "whatever happens tonight it won't be as bad as when I was booed off stage as Cher".

I stood up and briefly explained how I worked, I asked spirit to come in and guide me and with that we were off - the information started flowing. Before I knew it, Jan was calling time and the night was over, I had survived! Suddenly we had a huge round of applause, Jan pulled me to the side and said how well she felt I worked with my guides and it was lovely to see. She suggested I needed to work on projecting my voice a little bit more, but that would come with time.

Annette smiled and gave me a big hug saying, "I told you there was nothing to worry about". I thanked my guides, angels and helpers for working with me, and for not repeating the disaster at Worthing. I felt buzzed with the information spirit allowed me to pass on, Jan said "just think this is the worst you will ever be and look at the reaction and evidence you received. Trust within your sacred heart and you can never go wrong."

I felt for the first time in what seemed like forever this was my true calling. It felt different to when I performed as Cher. The drag show was all illusion everything was an escape a mask and creation of a character. The mediumship platform work was completely different. You were standing up in front of an audience exposing the truest and rawest version of yourself. If it went wrong, there was no one else to blame and nowhere to hide.

You had no script or lines to learn, you were stepping into the complete unknown. Until I stood up, I had no idea whom I would talk to and what might come out of my mouth - this did and still does scare the hell out of me. But in equal measure I knew my spirit team would be with me, delivering the goods as they had always done before. What was different was for the first time I completely surrendered my soul and allowed my spirit team in perhaps the closest they have ever been before. I put my complete trust into a higher power.

It felt amazing being able to channel evidence that our loved ones are safe, they do live on once the physical body dies.

I was lucky enough to meet Jan on several other occasions. Whilst she wasn't always in my life, she kind of was and I always felt her energy was around behind the scenes guiding me forward.

She believed in me the moment we met without question or condition. On our last encounter we met at Annette's Spiritual Summer Party that she hosted in her garden, Jan made a beeline for me as I was offering mini Tarot readings, so I consulted the cards and passed on what was being shown. She understood and said it all made sense.

She told me on this last meeting that she was quite ill and fighting a personal battle, she wasn't sure how long she had left on the earthly realm. She wanted to thank me for my gifts and I thanked her for seeing my light from the start. She reminded me to always trust the magic of spirit, and always remember the reason for being a voice box for the other world. With that she gave me a hug and off she went to mingle with everyone else. She was definitively a social butterfly.

This was sadly the last time I ever got to see her. But her knowledge and love, and belief has left a handprint on my heart forever. She taught me more about the spirit world in those brief times than I had previously ever learned from other places. Jan was a true earth angel but also a guardian angel. I have no question in my mind that she watches over myself and others that have been blessed to have her touch our hearts.

Mitch the Medium Up On Platform

Mr A

It really felt like I had a spring in my step, I was well and truly starting to walk my spiritual pathway. I was, however, very restricted due to working a forty-hour week in the bed shop, but I tried to do my spiritual work whenever possible.

About six months had gone by without a permanent store Manager but luckily for us the vacancy had finally been filled. The new Area Manager visited the store and welcomed us to (for purposes of this book we will call him Mr A, *A for Arsehole*) the new store Manager. (*Cheeky shout out..., I have also spoken in detail about Mr A in my first book "Timeless Magic - The Basic Book Of Spells"*).

Mr A was a middle-aged, bald, overweight, Scottish man, when I shook his hand, I felt a surge of fire pulsate through me. As a rule, I do try and get on with anyone - working in retail there is a high turnover of staff, and I met many different walks of life, and different colours of the rainbow. Mr A was on a whole new level I had not experienced before, we were opposite ends of the rainbow. I have referred to him in my other book as a Scottish Donald Trump, as this is exactly how his behaviour was. He was full of arrogance, ego, greed, homophobia, racism and he thought woman where beneath him and seemed to feel he was a cut above the rest.

Imagine shaking someone's hand and feeling dirty, that's how his energy made me feel every time I was in his presence. He had a typical Scottish fiery temper and the energy from him did not feel good at all. I knew he had been sent as another test from the spirit world. Was I going to allow yet another power-hungry idiot to take advantage? - it was it time to speak up.

My job over the coming months was to show him how to run the store day to day and train him on the managerial stuff. I said earlier I wasn't prepared to do anything beyond my job role and this was way beyond what was expected of me. But being the team-player I naturally was, I thought it easier to just get on with the task in hand, rather than rebel against it. Part of me really wanted to believe Mr A was going to be a great Manager and get the whole store back to some sort of normality. But the psychic in me already knew that was unachievable.

I spent time showing him the ropes, he didn't understand the way the business operated and suggested we make change, after change, after change. I tried to respect him as a Manager, but I had no respect for him as a person, he quickly tried to bring in sexual innuendos and would often ask me personal questions around my relationship. He seemed baffled that two men could be in love and have a respectful long-term relationship. I could feel he was jealous and didn't like the fact that my home life was for the most part really good.

We were getting nowhere fast, he was really struggling to take in basic information, admin duties and all the additional requirements for a Manager. Once more I was dealing with a salesperson with huge ego, thinking they were a lot better than they actually were. He would delight in telling me stories of how he was so successful in previous jobs and we were lucky to have him. I couldn't understand if he was at the height of his success why did he leave - his energy started to really drain me like a battery with no power left.

He had got 'wind' of my mediumship and Tarot work which was a subject I did not wish to discuss with him - he spent the following months dropping in little jibes and throwaway comments whenever he could.

One day we were quiet and he was really going on about my spiritual walk of life. He demanded for me to prove the existence of the spirit world, with that I felt the presence of my Nan and spirit team coming in close around me. "Show him" they were saying. Part of me wanted to just to shut him up, but the other part felt he didn't even deserve to see my gifts.

I felt the presence of his loved ones drawing in close and so passed on what they wanted him to know, his Mum stepped forward and I described how she looked, how she had passed and memory links they shared. I then brought through four other spirit family members and again, gave the validation they were channeling, he suddenly turned white like he had seen a ghost. He was in shock, it was like someone had smacked him around the face. For the first time since he had been here, he went quiet, there were no words…

"I need some air" he said and went outside pacing up and down the car park. He then phoned his girlfriend and I could hear him getting louder from outside in the car park. "How would he know all that stuff?" I heard him shouting down the phone to her. He came back in almost shaking and saying "OK, OK, maybe there is something more to life, but I don't want you to breathe a word of this to anyone". I explained to him that as a medium I couldn't care less if he believed me or not. That's not what the job of a medium is about – it is to simply pass on what spirit wish for you to know, what you go on to do with the information is up to you.

I would like to say this experience restored some balance and order, for a very short time maybe about a week it did, but then the fire he had within him seemed to amplify. After staying quiet for a couple of weeks and giving me some peace, something weird started happening. Whenever I missed out on sales targets, or add-ons etc., he seemed to try blaming it on my other lifestyle. "You have your head too far in the clouds" he would say. "I am going to performance manage you until you deliver the required results." This meant literally after every conversation with a customer he wanted feedback… Did they buy if not why? If they did buy, did they purchase a pillow, a ten-year guarantee, bedding etc. This was fast becoming a joke and once more I felt like I was on Dragon's Den or The Apprentice.

I feel at this stage he didn't like the fact I had a gift, and that it was something personal to me. He couldn't try and compete and say he had done it bigger and better, and that bothered him. For the first time he knew he had no power over me.

I Put A Spell on You

Over the next few months I tried to grit my teeth and bear the working relationship with Mr A. Often he would do the rota way ahead of time for the following month. I asked for two Saturdays per month off, as I was starting to book psychic fayres to read at and mind, body and spirit events. Nearly always when I asked for a particular date off, he would find a reason not to allow me to have it. "This is your job, and this must come first" used to be his reply. Numerous times I wanted to just hand my notice in and walk out on the spot, but my own pride and ego would not allow it. I was not prepared to leave because Mr A wanted to bully me out.

I continued to suffer in silence and had to pull out of events I had just paid for. This was not a good start I thought as people would think I was full of broken promises. On occasion I pulled a few sick days just so I could do the events I had signed up for.

Whilst at one fayre I got chatting to a fellow witch. "Why are you not working for yourself full time?" she said. I explained my situation and the nightmare I was having with Mr A. She asked whether I had used magic to try and resolve the situation. Up and till now I had not, and I felt a bit wary about doing so, for me my witchcraft was a very private personal experience. Whilst I was aware I could perform a spell to help, I really wanted the two worlds to stay separate.

She told me about an easy banishment spell I should try, and I told her I would think about it. For me, with my own witchcraft I felt and still do feel this way, that not everything can be fixed with magic. Sometimes there is learning within an experience even if you're not sure what the lesson is at the time. I was also aware that magic can be very hit and miss and can come with a cost, if not performed correctly.

Three days later I was chatting to my mentor and she also advised me of the same spell. This felt too weird to be coincidence, I explained to her my concerns with not wanting to do it. She simply said "sometimes we run out of hope or options with a person or situation, we hit a brick wall, and however much we will them to change, some people are just not ready to." I thought about this for a time, she was right, Mr A saw himself as perfect - he was never going to change, as for him there was nothing broken to fix.

Still a little unsure if I was doing the right thing I decided I needed to perform the spell for my own sanity. I took my time and cast the spell for the highest of good. Both my mentor and the fellow witch said to me, if cast correctly no harm will come to anyone. It will literally just shift and push the problem along its way. I waited not expecting too much, but hoping the spell would help, Mr A was doing my head in and it was time for him to go… if ever there was a time I needed some magic it was now!

Lady Luck must have been on my side, as two days later the spell only went and worked! The Area Manager came down to the store, and without rhyme or reason wanted a meeting with Mr A. announcing that with immediate effect Mr A would be working temporarily at the Swindon store. This made complete sense as he lived in Swindon, he said he wanted to help speed up and improve his product knowledge, I personally feel it was to try and show him how to manage a team correctly. Whatever the true reason was I didn't care I was just glad for a time he would be off my back. As soon as he left, the store felt calm and peaceful as it had always done prior to him being around. I thanked my spirit guides, angels and helpers for allowing the spell to work. The Area Manager said it will probably be for two months only.

This was perfect as it gave me time to start seriously looking for a new job. I was tidying the store one afternoon over the coming days and thinking about what life could be like. The store was dead and empty there was nobody around. Suddenly I saw in the door way the energy of my Nan "What are you doing?" she said to me in thought. "Why are you denying your own happiness?" I knew the spiritual walk of life was my calling, but I couldn't just leave with nothing to go to - I had rent, and bills to pay.

"Stop looking at your glass half-empty" she said, "there is no reason why anything should go wrong, you need to start seeing the true depth of the magic that lays within your heart. You are destined for something a lot more than this. Look around there is nothing here for you, no customers, no long-term opportunity. Give yourself permission to move forward and allow something better to come into your world. Give yourself the permission to be successful, but above all happy."

With that she faded away as quickly as she stepped forward, the room was full of unconditional love. She was right I was surviving in a world that didn't want me, I should be <u>living</u> life. The way spirit allowed me to feel when I passed a message onto someone was amazing, imagine if that could be my reality. What was actually blocking me? It wasn't Mr A or any of the other things I blamed, it was myself. I was preventing myself from being truly happy within my heart.

Brewing Up the Cauldron

Time to Say Goodbye

I spend the coming days pondering with the words of my Nan still freshly running within my head. Monday came along with Mr A temporarily out of the store and no performance reports would be done until he returned so I started looking at the report and the list of requirements. It was so silly, I honestly didn't care if I hit the targets or not, there was so much more to life, yet I felt almost trapped inside a goldfish bowl. Customers would press their face upon the glass, but it was 50/50 if they walked in - I didn't care how much I earned in commission or how much the store Manager made from me personally. For the first time it felt OK to not actually give a shit about any of it.

With that I pulled out a piece of paper and started writing my resignation letter. I faxed it to Head Office and the Area Manager, I wanted out of this world although I had no idea, where or what would await me. But I knew this had to come to an end and it was done, I was ready to leave but this time on my terms. As expected, the Area Manager tried to talk me into staying, my contract said I had to give a month's notice, I gave them two weeks, I didn't care if I lost out on some commission I just wanted out, what was the worst that could happen, they sack me!

That two weeks felt like the slowest of my life, I spent most of it job hunting and applying for things online.

Finally, the morning of my last day arrived - it couldn't have come any sooner! I had my morning coffee and saw there was a voicemail on my phone. It was one of the jobs I had applied for wanting to meet with me today for an interview, I was working with the part-timer and told him the situation. The job was only in Melksham so not far from Trowbridge at all, "Go over" he said, "I can hold the fort, if anyone asks, I'll say you have nipped out to a customer's house as they have a problem with their bed."

This was perfect, I phoned the person at the new job back and said I could be there within the hour. Off I went. I didn't really know what to think or expect as this job was worlds apart from the bed shop. It was a factory environment packing second hand books for online orders - I arrived and was greeted by a rather eccentric gentleman and rather than an interview we had a very, very informal chat. I didn't want my spiritual walk of life to be an issue and so I told him from the off what I did. "Brilliant" he said, "I have healing a lot myself, so I completely understand this world." I was shocked for the first time ever in my working world someone understood and was encouraging of my alternative work. We carried on chatting and without warning he said you have the job start Monday.

Wow, had it really been as easy as that? I remember what my Nan had said "don't view your cup has half empty."

I decided to go the long way home and stopped off at McDonalds before I went back to the bed shop for the last time. I was buzzing, new doorways were opening in front of me without me needing to do very much at all it seemed.

When I got back, I explained I had been offered the job there and then, still the hours dragged by until it was finally time to leave. I handed over my keys, clocked out for the last time, and let the part-timer lock the store behind me. He shook my hand and wished me well with all I turned my hand to in the future. As I went to my car, I looked over my shoulder and it felt like the weight of the world had been lifted. I was officially free from the nightmare job and for the first time in what felt like forever, I could breathe again.

Waking Up to a New World

Paranormal Activity

I started my new job on the Monday, it was on a temporary to permanent basis. This was perfect for me, no targets, no uniform, literally turn up and do the work and then go home. The team was made up of eight to ten people, most of them younger than me, in their early twenties. I decided that I wasn't going to broadcast my spiritual work, but I certainly wasn't going to hide it either.

The job was very easy, and I was warned I might get bored quickly, in the warehouse there was row upon row of all different books on shelves, it was like a huge library. In the morning on arrival any orders would be printed off. You had a hand gun that scanned the barcode of the book and the job was simply to find the book that matched the order. We all had our own desk space to box the orders up and when this was done, they would go out onto a pallet truck awaiting delivery. This was so easy I thought, whilst the job was very basic, I loved it.

As well as getting on with the work, the newbies often were subjected to pranks being played upon them. I had only been there five minutes and already I hadn't laughed this much in years, it really highlighted to me just how unhappy I had previously been.

In the afternoon, when all the orders were complete, we had to book in and put out new stock, we were often put into small groups for this between two and three people per group depending on how many orders came in. "Put Mitch's group upstairs" someone said... Some of the guys were trying to make out that it was the oldest and more scary part of the building. The people within my team seemed a little nervous but agreed. I started to laugh thinking this must be a prank they had planned, I was happy to go along as the spirit world hadn't scared me yet, in my experience it was the <u>living</u> you had to watch out for.

My group went upstairs and straight away I could feel a change in temperature and energy. Now normally hot air rises, but I felt instantly cold and almost as if I was being watched, I thought to myself more than likely someone is going to jump out on me up here. But I was open to what they had planned, it was all part of the fun and if it made the day go a little quicker, I was happy to part take in whatever prank was in store. I started to run my eyes along the rows of books, oh yes, I was indeed within my element up here. I suddenly found old books on witchcraft and the occult. Around the corner there was rows of oracle and Tarot cards. Books on crystals, UFOs and all things paranormal and other worldly - it almost felt like I had been guided up to this area. As I continued along allowing my eyes to scan taking in all the exciting goodies on the shelf. One of my group shouted out "Mitch don't go too far back there, there is something we need to tell you". They then went on to say how this section of the warehouse was extremely haunted. I started laughing to myself, as none of them knew what I did.

The good thing about older books is that the shelves had slightly more depth so if you looked through you could see the next three rows. I looked through and three rows ahead I could see one of the guys from the other group hiding waiting to jump out on me. 'Hmm time to debunk the prank' I thought so I sneaked along the rows and knowing what row number he was on, I was able to hide a row behind him. I went to the far end and just happened to find a thick book on the paranormal, I gently pushed it off the shelf 'boom' it made a huge bang as it hit the floor. My colleague jumped out of his skin, he had his back directly to where I was hiding. The factory fell silent, 'BOO!' I suddenly said loudly. He literally jumped out of his skin causing me to laugh hysterically. 'That will teach you to try and jump out on me you little shit' I thought to myself. The group rejoined, and everyone started laughing their heads off. Because I had stood my ground and out-pranked the prankster it was like they all wanted to be around me, and I had earned my place within the factory.

Normal service resumed, and it was decided that my team would stay upstairs and work in that area. I spent the time whenever possible reading through the various books. Often the oracle decks and Tarot cards would be unsealed so I would quickly play with the decks and pick a quick card for the week ahead. No matter which deck I used they always gave timely advice.

One day I was up there putting stock away, suddenly I felt the presence of someone with me. 'Hmm great another prank' I thought and carried on putting stock away. A book at the end of my row fell onto the floor. Now the girls in the factory had a habit of throwing books over the shelf so at first, I thought it was one of them up there messing about. Very funny. I went and picked up the book, strange it was grey, very battered up looking, with no title. I placed it back on the shelf and carried on, two minutes later the same book came off the shelf again. 'Hmm ok someone is defiantly up here messing around wanting to prank me' I thought. As I was going off to headcount where everyone was the rest of my group suddenly appeared. Where have you guys been? "Out for a vape" they said… "what's up?". "So, none of you have been up here throwing books around?" Now the girls tended to struggle to keep a straight face if a prank was happening, but they said that no one had been up there with me. I felt into the energy and tried to feel if any actual spirits were about. I had become very good and keeping myself closed and putting boundaries in place at this new job.

Next all of us went to the middle section of the upstairs warehouse, this was good as you could roughly see down every aisle. We started to get the next lot of books to put into stock and whilst this was happening I suddenly asked my spirit team to come in close around me. If anyone was here I wanted to know. With that we all saw out of the corner of our eyes something run down the third aisle… I could feel the energy of the warehouse changing and the presence of spirit coming in. Somebody or something was indeed with us…

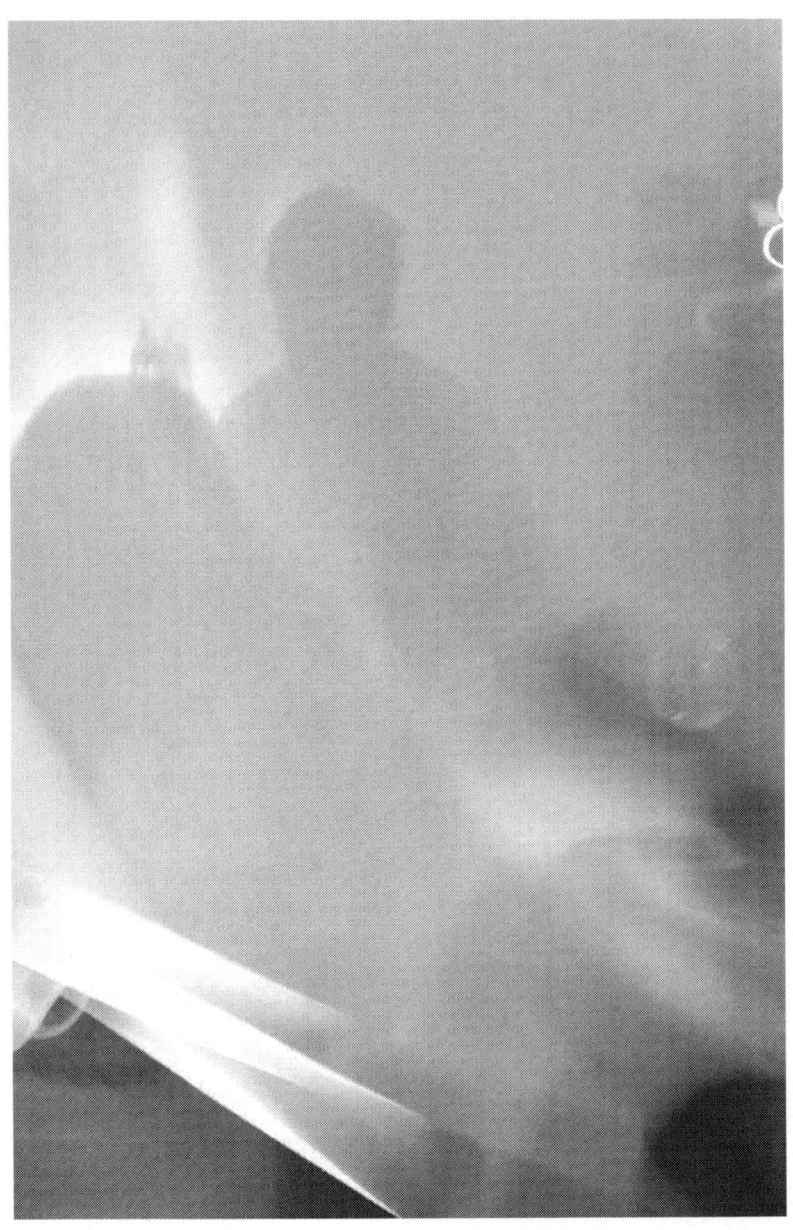

Taken on a Photo Shoot Showing Spirit Activity

A Girl Called Amelia

I decided it was time to let the team know what I did in my spare time, without questioning it too much I told them in a matter of fact way that I was a spiritual Medium. They all started freaking out thinking it was the coolest thing ever, some of the guys where immediately sceptical and got a bit cross that I said about it. I didn't have time to worry about their thoughts on the subject.

I told then I was aware there is a spirit up here wanting to connect with us and instantly felt a feeling of entrapment. I felt this spirit was a friendly young girl aged around five or six, I also knew that she knew I could feel or sense that she was there. The girls in the group started saying "before you joined, we refused to work this section of the warehouse as it scared us. Often we felt like we had heard noises and whisperings." One of the girls went on to say she felt her hair had been pulled a few times. But thought perhaps she had just caught it on the shelving?

They all started asking who or what is was, I explained there was too much hustle and bustle to fully connect. Whilst I could feel the energy of this spirit girl, she made me feel she liked to scare the girls, but she only wanted to play with them. I felt she was very wary around men and she was making me feel there was a real darkness to her passing.

I almost felt because she had been born a girl her father had not wanted her, and I feel he was disappointed she had not been a boy and perhaps the reason she passed over. She gave me the feeling of being drowned or thrown into a water well. I said I need to earn her trust, that she knows I am her to help her if that's what she would like. I said to the group "Let's gets back to work and I'll see if she can link with me." I wasn't able to get her to link right away and as quick as she came in off she went.

In the days that followed there was a bit of an odd atmosphere in the air, the whole factory had started to talk about me and my 'gifts'. Some of the girls were very open and intrigued and a few of the guys were too. But there was also a group that wouldn't embrace and refused to accept there was a spirit world or afterlife. I tried to explain my job as a medium was never to force or make a person believe but a lot of hostility was thrown my way. Once again, I was quickly feeling like an outsider looking in on the edge of a circle that didn't want me.

The boss asked me to go to his office for an informal chat, as he had heard all the gossip going on. I thought "Great I had only been here a short while and was going to be in big trouble". We sat down, and he started to talk. "I know you can do what you do, and I am also aware of the girl upstairs. I have never said anything as I didn't want to scare anyone. Are you able to help her without everyone knowing about it?" I told him I could try and send her to the light if I can gain her trust. He asked me "Do what you need to do but please don't allow the staff to get wind of this". I was shocked and humbled he seemed to have a genuine respect for the spirit world, and my own gifts. He asked me if there are any others and I told him I hadn't connected with any. He told me that he himself had had some strange experiences whilst upstairs and then he called time on the meeting and I went back to my stack of books.

It was proposed that me and my small group stay upstairs so we could do our work and I could do the spirit work without scaring the rest of the group. Easier said than done I thought as I knew that this was going to all be on spirit's terms.

I decided that the best plan was for me to go off alone and focus on the areas far back within the warehouse, where some of the previous activity had occurred. I started asking for the little girl in spirit to step forward and if she was able to connect. I wanted to keep the experience friendly and gentle, like if you were greeting someone on the earth plane. I started putting my books on to the shelf and asked, "what's your name little one?" Like a radio being tuned in I started to hear whisperings… I couldn't quite make the name out? Amanda? Amy? I just couldn't hear it properly.

With that a book three rows along pushed itself forward but not completely off the shelf, the spine was exposed, and I went to look at it. The book was an old brown fabric material, it had a beautiful gold embossed font, and it simply said the name Amelia. Amelia, I thought that is your name. I walked back to my stack of books and said, "If Amelia is your name give me a sign." With that the same book ever so gently fell off the shelf and onto the floor. There was no big bang like last time. Just a small gentle thud. OK, I thought, we have a name...

I spent the coming days trying to connect with Amelia, but nothing happened. I could sense she was there, but she still was refusing to connect deeply. I decided to carry on being an open line of channel and I started asking my spirit guides for more information and how I could help her. My own spirit team told me she wants to find her Mum but fears her Father. He had blood on his hands and was the reason she passed over, just as I had felt the first time she stepped forward.

Days went on, and I kept talking in thought to Amelia when I knew she was around and listening. I told her she didn't need to hide amongst the books and she was ready to travel to the light. My spirit guides assured me her Mum is trying to find her and they will connect, I was almost the jigsaw piece my guides said to make this happen. I was feeling a bit disheartened I wanted desperately to help her, but knew she had to do it for herself.

Friday afternoon came around, I felt energy around me but again I couldn't pinpoint Amelia in as close as I knew she was able to connect. The guys were all up helping the team, we had a big order turn up and it had to be finished before we could leave. It was a case of all hands on deck.

"Been doing any ghostbusting lately?" one of the non-believers said causing the whole warehouse to laugh hysterically. 'Whatever' I thought, I wasn't interested in getting caught up in their ignorance or garbage, with that on about the fourth row along one of the guys that did believe suddenly screamed my name. "Mitch come here quick!". "What is it?" I shouted out. I can see a girl sitting on the floor. She is wearing a dress and has her back on the bookshelf with her knees up. "Have you got your phone handy?" "Yes" he said and with that he started snapping away. I knew by the time I got there she would be gone. "What does she look like?" I asked, he said it was like a dark shadow or tracing paper, he could see her but also see through her!

I made my way to the aisle he was on and sure enough she had vanished. We started looking through the photos on his iPhone, it was hard to make out at first. He added on a black and white filter, 'boom' there she was plain as day in the image. 'Perfect' I thought, this was big validation that she was testing us to see what she could get away with, but I also knew we were starting to earn her trust. The non-believers within the group demanded to look at the photo, despite taking a few shots she was only captured in one. They started saying they couldn't see anything but then the others started to highlight her outline. 'So much for keeping it quiet' I thought, 'nice one Amelia'. The boss came out of his office as he heard all the drama unfolding. He gave me a look as if to say "I thought we had an agreement." I did say sorry and that it was outside of my control.

Home time came, and I was getting my stuff together and one of the last to leave. The boss came out and said "Come in an hour earlier on Monday morning please. I feel Amelia will be waiting for you." With that he wished me a good weekend and that was that.

On Monday I was a bit unsure about having to come in a whole hour early, but I did as I was instructed as I felt I was in a sea of drama and wanted to try and resolve it as quickly as possible. The boss welcomed me in to the factory saying, "I often see her on the stairs, I'll be in my office - let me know what happens." With that he left me alone in the warehouse. The lights had only just turned on and took time to fully charge and become bright. I walked around the half-lit warehouse, often full of laughter and banter, for the first time it felt a bit creepy and just not quite right.

I went to the staircase and before I had a chance to climb the stairs. Amelia was standing there on the middle step looking at me. Whilst I wasn't scared for the first time she did make me jump. "It's time to go little one" I said, "your Mum is looking for you." With that I asked for her energy to move on to the light, the roof of the warehouse started to shine with brilliant pure white light, as bright as the sun. I have never seen anything quite like it before. I felt her spirit rise off the step and she started to float up almost like a mystical smoke. Suddenly the place fell silent, the beam of light had gone, and the roof was once more a dull grey with cobwebs everywhere whilst the upper part of the warehouse felt warm, light and cosy.

The boss came to tell me that it was nearly time for everyone else to start to arrive. I had walked up the stairs by this time and was looking out over the warehouse from the balcony. "She has gone home hasn't she?". I told him I thought she had and he said he could also feel the change in energy. He thanked me and told me this had been a long time coming.

I went around the rows of books and made my way to the back of the warehouse. The rows didn't feel full of unease or apprehension anymore and a feeling of calm and peace washed over me. I went to the bookshelf where the big old fabric book was sitting neatly in its row. I gently started to pull out the book titled Amelia, as I went to pull this out the tiniest white feather was sitting on the top of the spine. A smile washed over me, for I knew this was a sign from Amelia, she was home safe and now in the realm of unconditional love. The spirit world. My spirit team whispered in thought to me 'your work here is done…'

The Photo Taken of Amelia Sitting Against The Book Shelf

Stranger in This World

As time went on the warehouse went back to normality. Amelia did not try to reconnect, and the upstairs continued to feel warm and loved. Christmas was approaching, usually a busy period for most businesses, however that was not the case here. The weeks rolled on and the bosses kept talking about how we were about to hit peak trading season. We waited patiently but the peak didn't seem to arrive and eventually an emergency meeting was called. Before we sat down, I knew what was coming as I had been in this position before.

    The boss told us that due to poor sales this year, four of us are going to be asked to leave the business. We all went in one by one and he explained it was nothing personal, he had to keep the staff that had been with him long term. I went in to hear what he had to say, and he gently closed the door. He said "First of all thank you so much, you are one of the top workers here, and thank you for sending Amelia home, if there was a way to keep you on I would. But you are also very different from the rest, you have a rare gift that should be shared with the greater world." He was a very free-spirited man. "The earth needs your energy to help it heal and love again. You are a light worker. Did you know Mitch…. that, Earth and Heart are spelt the same way?" Being dyslexic 'no' I hadn't made the connection. You have had some fun here, it was a fun little holiday period, but it's now clear your real work is ready to begin.

The words of the medium all those years ago at the bed shop once more rang in my ears. But this time, I believed I knew what my real work was. He wished me well and hoped our paths would cross again, but he also said he knew I was about to open up a doorway to a brand-new adventure that would change lives. He gave me a gentle hug and with that he opened the door, and I was once again free to leave.

I gathered my stuff together, some others who had been asked to leave were getting very hostile and upset. They asked me if I was angry or pissed off as they thought I should be, 'I should be' I thought, it was approaching Christmas and I had bills and rent to pay. I said, "No, it's nothing personal it's the way it's meant to be." With that I bid everyone farewell and wished them luck and I made my way out of the warehouse. I looked on and smiled because I realised I was never sent here to do the work of the others, my purpose was always to help send Amelia over to the light.

I drove home and explained to Paul what had happened. He started to panic, 'how are we going to live? This is the worst time of year to be out of work?' I let him carry on pacing up and down and gave him time to get to grips with the news.

I had felt my body wake up and become alive with magic, I was no longer interested in how much money I had sitting in my bank account or how much I had to sell to get a huge monthly bonus. For the first time none of it mattered. It was all illusion, conditioning to keep a person small and in their place. I was blessed in so many other ways, I had good health, a partner who loves me, family and friends that love me, a roof over my head, clean clothing, food in my belly, I already had all the riches I needed - I was indeed blessed.

I felt the power of the earth and spirit world coming in close around me. "It is time to unplug yourself from the matrix system" I could hear them say. "It is time to not only survive but live and be present in a world where you answer to no one but yourself. It does not matter if anyone believes in you or not, for you yourself are now standing in your own light of truth. That is the real gift and the most powerful magic a person can own."

I spent the coming days feeling I was just going to put myself out there as a psychic advisor, I looked into the online companies wanting readers. I went through numerous test readings and passed on all of them, yet something felt imbalanced and altogether not right.

It didn't feel ethical for me to be a reader online and have people pay £1.00 up to £3.00 per minute - not only that I would only receive 30% of the takings - I wasn't prepared to burn myself out anymore for someone else's personal gain.

I decided instead to walk the pathway alone. I made up a very basic website and launched myself as a spiritual medium, psychic and tarot reader. I decided to charge a middle of the road price and one I would be happy to pay myself.

I didn't really have any immediate expectations, and I wasn't sure what would come of it. When we are ready to walk our true purpose, calling or journey, like stepping stones the road becomes clear. There was no one blocking me, or standing in my way, I was ready to walk the next stage of my journey. The pathway started to present itself in my line of vision.

It was time to walk with the spirit world…

Inspiration

Until You're Ready to Look Foolish, You'll Never Have the Possibility of Being Great – *Cher*

My Cher Tattoo is Very Symbolic - it represents the amazing adventures as a performer but also the magick of the spirit world.

Acknowledgements

I want to thank the following people, as without your help love and support this book would have not been possible.

Sharon Chalk - Editor

Heather Stark - Front cover illustration
www.facebook.com/Witchward-Bound-378516335867496

Annette Geering - Mediumship - Tarot - Meditation - Hypnotherapy
www.enchantedtarot.co.uk
www.enlighteninghypnotherapysolutions.co.uk

Shining Light Westbury - Development - Mediumship Nights
www.facebook.com/shininglightwestbury/

Printed in Great
Britain
by Amazon